CUBA

A Publication of the Americas  Society

CUBA

The Contours of Change

edited by
Susan Kaufman Purcell
David J. Rothkopf

LYNNE
RIENNER
PUBLISHERS

BOULDER
LONDON

Published in the United States of America in 2000 by
Lynne Rienner Publishers, Inc.
1800 30th Street, Boulder, Colorado 80301
www.rienner.com

and in the United Kingdom by
Lynne Rienner Publishers, Inc.
3 Henrietta Street, Covent Garden, London WC2E 8LU

Library of Congress Cataloging-in-Publication Data
Cuba : the contours of change / edited by Susan Kaufman Purcell
and David Rothkopf.
  Includes bibliographical references and index.
  ISBN 1-55587-933-0 (pbk. : alk. paper)
  1. Cuba—Economic conditions—1990– 2. Cuba—Politics and government—
1959– 3. Cuba—Foreign economic relations—United States. 4. United States—
Foreign economic relations—Cuba. I. Purcell, Susan Kaufman. II. Rothkopf,
David J. (David Jochanan), 1955–
  HC152.5.C7984   2000
  330.97291—dc21   00-031093

British Cataloguing in Publication Data
A Cataloguing in Publication record for this book
is available from the British Library.

Printed and bound in the United States of America

      The paper used in this publication meets the requirements
 ∞   of the American National Standard for Permanence of
      Paper for Printed Library Materials Z39.48-1984.

      5 4 3 2 1

Contents

Foreword

No other foreign policy issues in the United States are debated as regularly or hotly as those involving Cuba. Our neighbors in the hemisphere and our friends in Europe scratch their heads in wonder at the attention Fidel Castro gets in U.S. politics. Far from subsiding since the end of the Cold War, the debate, if anything, has intensified. Castro ensured this by attacking the embargo and creating incidents to highlight the "threat" to his regime. On the U.S. side, deep-seated emotions and high domestic political stakes keep the issues front and center.

Although the attention paid to U.S.-Cuban relations has been intense, the heat generated tends to obscure the degree of change that has taken place in Cuba over the past decade. Castro has aged; the economy has deteriorated in the absence of Soviet subsidies; social programs have suffered; the island's technological level has slid backward. In an attempt to stem the crisis, the regime has experimented fitfully with economic reforms, but infrastructure breakdowns and the stop-and-go pace of reform have caused popular frustration and complaints. Meanwhile, oppression and human-rights violations continue. Important questions face the United States as it grapples with these changes: What will happen when Castro departs the scene? What should the United States be doing to accelerate his departure and best position itself for the post-Castro era? The urgency of these questions provides a strong reason for the United States to take a cool, fresh

look at the issues as we enter a new decade, with evolving relationships between the United States and its neighbors to the south and a
new administration coming to Washington.

Representing a wide range of political views, the authors and
editors of this book present an up-to-date examination of U.S. policy options toward Cuba and the complex considerations that under-
lie those options. One focus of the book is the political reality on the
island, a reality marked by a mix of strong forces for change and
powerful interests favoring the status quo. This reality leaves considerable uncertainty about what will follow Castro, especially with
few national institutions strong enough to guide events. The authors
also look at the economic crisis facing Cuba, as well as the economic potential of the island. After Castro is gone, is a market economy likely to develop? If so, will there be important commercial opportunities for U.S. business, as some contend?

The future of the embargo is also addressed. On the one hand,
the fact that dollar remittances by Cuban exiles and Cuban Americans are the largest hard-currency inflows to the regime suggests a
major flaw in the embargo policy. On the other hand, ending the
embargo in the hope that U.S. commerce and influence will effect
fundamental changes in the regime suggests the United States may
underestimate how *cabeziduro* (stubborn) Castro is and will be disillusioned if change does not come. Both the pro- and anti-embargo
arguments and their underlying assumptions are detailed in separate
chapters.

This book does not pretend to arrive at a new policy proposal.
Nor does it provide one unified answer to the question of where U.S.
interests lie in dealing with Castro. Rather, the authors advocate different approaches based on their own experience and judgment. In
the process, they provide readers with the information needed to arrive at their own decision about what kind of policy responds best to
the interests of the United States and those of the Cuban people.

Thomas E. McNamara
President, Americas Society

Acknowledgments

This book is the result of the combined efforts of a number of individuals and organizations. We especially would like to thank the members of the 1999 study group "Cuba: Preparing for the Future," who contributed their expertise and insights regarding Cuba's present political and economic situation and the country's prospects for becoming a democracy and a market economy.

We would particularly like to thank Marianne Benet, assistant to the vice president of the Americas Society, for her invaluable assistance in organizing the study group and preparing the resulting manuscript for publication. We would also especially like to thank Ben Ramsey, associate program officer at the Americas Society, for coordinating and running the study group. Thanks also go to Eliav Decter, former assistant to the vice president, and Alex Gross, former associate program officer, for their help in the initial phases of the project. In addition, we wish to thank Michelle Miller-Adams for her excellent editorial work. Finally, we would like to acknowledge the staff at Lynne Rienner Publishers for their valuable contributions to the editorial and publication processes.

This book and the study group from which it developed were made possible by a generous grant to the Western Hemisphere Department of the Americas Society by the Tinker Foundation, Inc. We especially wish to thank the foundation's chair, Martha T. Muse, and its president, Renate Rennie, for their continuing support.

Susan Kaufman Purcell
David J. Rothkopf

Acronyms
and Abbreviations

ACS	Association of Caribbean States
ALADI	Latin American Integration Association
CADECA	currency exchange (*Casa de Cambio*)
CANF	Cuban American National Foundation
Caricom	Caribbean Community
CEPAL	Economic Commission for Latin America and the Caribbean (United Nations)
CTC	Confederation of Cuban Workers
ETA	Euzkadi ta Askatasuna (Basque Fatherland and Freedom)
FAR	Revolutionary Armed Forces
FARC	Revolutionary Armed Forces of Colombia
FDI	foreign direct investment
FTZ	free-trade zone
GDP	gross domestic product
GNP	gross national product
IRELA	Institute for European–Latin American Relations
Mercosur	Common Market of the South
NAFTA	North American Free Trade Agreement
NGO	nongovernmental organization
NAPP	National Assembly of Popular Power
PRI	Institutional Revolutionary Party (Mexico)
PSP	Popular Socialist Party
WTO	World Trade Organization

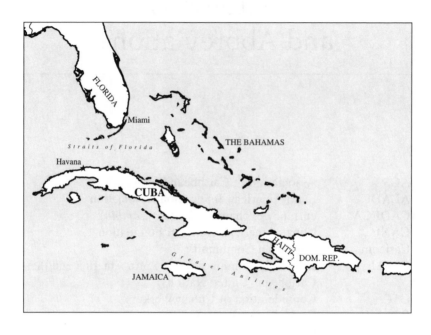

Cuba

1

Cuba:
The Shape of Things to Come

William M. LeoGrande

The contributors to this volume on contemporary Cuba have spent many years studying the island and its socialist experiment. Here, they not only present a snapshot of Cuba's immediate circumstances—which are difficult, to say the least—but also attempt to look ahead, giving the reader some guideposts for understanding where Cuba is going and how it is likely to get there.

Not surprisingly, the authors' views often differ, but each of them offers a well-reasoned, plausible vision of things to come. That they disagree so sharply on some points is testimony to the difficulty social scientists have in making predictions about Cuba, where so much still depends on the decisions of the *líder máximo,* who has on occasion changed his mind and abruptly reversed course. Indeed, one point of contention among these authors is exactly how much control Fidel Castro has over the crisis that engulfed Cuba after the end of the Cold War. How much is he still able to direct events, and how much is he being swept along by them, staying afloat by accommodating the new reality of global capitalism rather than resisting it?

The task of comprehending Cuba is also complicated by the emotions surrounding it, not just for Cuban Americans, but for anyone who takes an interest in U.S. foreign policy and relations with our nearby neighbors. Antagonism toward Cuba has been at the center of U.S. hemispheric policy since Dwight D. Eisenhower was president, and Washington's stance has always been contentious at home. Much has

changed in the world since the 1960s, but the debate over Cuba remains astonishingly similar today to what it was in the aftermath of the
missile crisis.[1] Does engagement or isolation hold more promise for
safeguarding U.S. interests and for promoting change in Cuba? In this
volume are briefs for both sides—intelligent, moderate, and yet utterly
at odds with one another.

The Transition from Socialism

U.S. policy toward Cuba may be frozen in time, but on the island things
have changed dramatically since the end of the Cold War. Andrew
Zimbalist and Manuel Pastor Jr. provide harrowing accounts of the
damage done to the Cuban economy by the collapse of communism in
Eastern Europe and the Soviet Union. Not only did Cuba conduct about
85 percent of its trade with these partners before 1989, it also received
preferential prices equivalent to several billion dollars of aid annually.
Without these subsidies, Cuba's capacity to import shrank by 75 percent, causing severe shortages of energy, raw materials, and food. The
resulting depression slashed gross domestic production (GDP) by at
least 35 percent, led to the closure of hundreds of factories, and left
tens of thousands of Cubans unemployed. By one estimate, real wages
shrank 80 percent between 1989 and 1995.

The government's response to this crisis came in two phases. The
first was a short-term strategy that aimed to reorient trade relations
toward the West, attract foreign investment to substitute for the lost
subsidies, and produce enough food to avert serious malnutrition. The
hallmark of this strategy was that it sought to weather the immediate
crisis without undertaking any significant domestic economic reforms.
By late 1993, the inadequacy of this approach had become clear; the
crisis was deepening rather than abating. Thus, the second phase of
policy changes included a series of market-oriented reforms, among
them the reestablishment of free farmers' markets, the devolution of
many state farms to cooperatives, sharp reductions in subsidies to state
enterprises, the legalization of self-employment, and—most significantly—the legalization of U.S. dollars.

There is no doubt that Fidel Castro authorized these changes with
the greatest reluctance. In oft-repeated public declarations, he has
lamented the need to make concessions to the market, denounced the

negative social effects of market-oriented change, and reaffirmed his commitment to socialism.[2] By condemning the new policies as he undertakes them, Castro has raised doubts about whether the changes made in the Cuban economy are permanent or merely temporary expedients to be dropped as soon as macroeconomic conditions permit. Even the significance of the changes made thus far is debatable. Susan Kaufman Purcell, Jaime Suchlicki, and David J. Rothkopf regard them as relatively inconsequential; Andrew Zimbalist and Manuel Pastor Jr. see them as having had more profound and lasting effects. All agree, however, that the policies undertaken to date do not amount to a Cuban transition to capitalism.

Purcell, Suchlicki, and Rothkopf contend (implicitly at least) that, although Cuba's reform program is insufficient to stimulate long-term growth, it seems to have stabilized the economy and can be continued in its current configuration more or less indefinitely. Politics are in command. If Castro is determined to hold the line against further reforms, he will. If he decides to roll back the reforms already made, he can.

Economists Pastor and Zimbalist, on the other hand, see Cuba's limited reforms as unsustainable. Because the cocoon of the socialist trading bloc no longer cushions Cuba's export-oriented economy, Cuba must trade in the world market at world market prices. Its external-sector industries must produce efficiently to be competitive. Can Cuba maintain a fire wall between the external sector and the domestic economy? Can it sustain an inefficient state sector indefinitely? Neither Pastor nor Zimbalist thinks so. They argue that current reforms do not go far enough, cannot generate long-term growth, and must inevitably fail. The emerging distortion of income distribution is one symptom of how dysfunctional existing policies have become. As Zimbalist says, "Material rewards in Cuba today do not correspond in any meaningful way with one's economic contribution." Cubans with access to dollars (those who work in an externally oriented industry or those with relatives abroad who send them remittances) have become a highly privileged group. Not only are many consumer goods available only for dollars, but the average wage rate is a few hundred pesos a month, whereas the peso-to-dollar exchange rate has stabilized at about twenty to one. Consequently, even highly paid Cuban professionals have a powerful incentive to quit their jobs and chase the *Yanqui* dollar.

Zimbalist's verdict on this state of affairs is stark: "Cuba's present model is simply no longer viable. The longer it is rigidly pursued, the more likely it is that the present system will come to a violent and destructive end." The only alternative is an aggressive program of reform that stimulates the nascent private sector (which has been the sole source of growth in recent years) and effectively privatizes the state sector by turning state enterprises into cooperatives. For Pastor, the alternatives are a gradual process of transition to a market economy that cushions the impact on ordinary Cubans, or the "shock therapy" of a rapid transition, with the attendant risk of political instability. He, too, concludes that Cuba must inevitably replace state socialism with capitalism, albeit, he hopes, a capitalism that retains some of Cuba's social-welfare system.

The conundrum, of course, is how the economic imperative for reform that Zimbalist and Pastor identify will be translated through the Cuban political system. Most of the authors doubt that an augmented reform program is on the horizon. As Jaime Suchlicki points out in his review of the Cuban political scene, Castro's regime is relatively stable. There are no discernible fissures in the party or the military. Fidel Castro's unrivaled authority mutes elite divisions over how to respond to the current crisis. Popular discontent is expressed through passive resistance or emigration rather than by organized opposition, which is quickly repressed whenever it appears. A program of real economic reform, however, could prove politically dangerous, leading to an "erosion of political power and control." Castro will not undertake real reform, despite the ongoing economic problems. Suchlicki concludes that the regime is stable enough to "muddle through" indefinitely with poor but sustainable economic performance, even into a post-Castro era.

Purcell and Rothkopf essentially agree that Castro is unlikely to accept the inevitability of capitalism and act as the midwife of its rebirth in Cuba. Zimbalist, while arguing that the survival of the Cuban regime depends upon profound economic change, acknowledges that the government is hostile toward policies that would further strengthen the emerging private sector. He refrains from speculating on how the political elite might come to change its view, therefore leaving the reader with the most implicitly pessimistic forecast—that political intransigence will lead to a social explosion.

Pastor's assessment is less pessimistic. In thinking through the politics of economic transition, Pastor argues that even the limited reforms undertaken thus far "have opened some space for new social forces that might be more interested in reform." The obvious groups are small farmers (both on private farms and in cooperatives), who benefit from the free market in agricultural commodities, and self-employed urban entrepreneurs. This emerging private sector has been the target of Fidel Castro's harshest criticism, and he is clearly loath to allow it to thrive. Even within the governing elite, however, there are pragmatic managers responsible for solving real problems, who constitute a force for change. Managers of joint ventures and externally oriented industries are already having to adapt to market discipline. As subsidies for state enterprises dry up, other Cuban managers will also be forced to adapt and will presumably press for government policies that make their jobs easier. Nor can the pressure of popular opinion be discounted entirely; after all, it was the depth of discontent in 1993–1994 that led the government to embark on the path of reform in the first place.

Are there the makings of a reform coalition in this collection of inchoate social groups? Perhaps, but at the same time one should not discount the political strength of those who might resist more thoroughgoing change. As both Zimbalist and Pastor point out, reform of the highly inefficient state sector will generate significant unemployment. Cuban trade unions have already been complaining, albeit discreetly, about the limited reforms undertaken thus far. They represent a large constituency that could become a formidable conservative force opposing more market-oriented policies, as happened in some Eastern European countries. Pastor worries that unless the government undertakes a gradual transition that cushions the hardships associated with economic restructuring, popular support for change may prove unsustainable. The party bureaucracy, as Suchlicki notes, is another bastion of the status quo, since its power and its ideological raison d'être would disappear with the passing of the planned economy.

At present, Fidel Castro appears to have decided against further reforms, and that settles the issue for the time being. But is his government's monopoly on political power eroding along with its control over the economy? To some degree, the answer is unquestionably yes, but the long-term significance of the erosion is a matter of conjecture, and hence dispute. Castro clearly dislikes and distrusts the emerging private entrepreneurial class, but the government cannot do without its productivity, expansion of employment opportunities, or tax revenues (all of which the state sector fails to provide). Thus the government must put up with people whose self-interest places them in conflict with it—over tax rates, regulations, supply distribution, and, ultimately, fundamental ideology.

In the past few years, the government has also reached a modus vivendi with the Catholic Church, which has swelled in popularity. The church is in the process of developing an infrastructure of religious, social, and charitable groups across the island—the only such organizational structure that is not state controlled. As Suchlicki points out, the church is careful not to challenge the regime too directly. But it does occasionally voice criticism of state policies, especially on human rights, and it thereby constitutes living proof that one can be a loyal Cuban, not a pawn of the United States, and still disagree with Fidel Castro. This is a significant change in Cuban political culture.

Finally, there has been a proliferation of nongovernmental organizations in recent years. Most are government approved, which makes Suchlicki skeptical that they constitute a real flowering of civil society. But they are a new phenomenon, nevertheless, and a channel through which a growing number of Cubans will come into contact with people and ideas from abroad. Some of these groups are at least independent enough to have aroused the government's suspicion.[3]

Suchlicki is right when he concludes that none of these changes have significantly diminished the regime's authoritarian control as of yet. Purcell is right, too, when she warns against the "economic determinism" of assuming that the opening of markets inevitably produces a decentralization of political control. Looking forward, it is impossible to predict whether these developments on the margin of the Cuban polity represent mere epiphenomena or the front edge of a growing tide of change. Fidel Castro still makes Cuban history, but even he cannot make it just as he pleases.

The Bad Neighbor Policy

Why is Cuba still such a sore spot for the United States? As David J. Rothkopf points out in Chapter 6, the main reason Washington was preoccupied with Cuba during the 1960s, 1970s, and 1980s was national security. Cuba was an ally of our global adversary and sought to advance Soviet foreign policy at the expense of U.S. interests. Fidel Castro was an avid and active player on the world stage, promoting revolution in Latin America and Africa; sending troops to fight for the cause of proletarian internationalism in Syria, Angola, and Ethiopia; and leading the Movement of Nonaligned Nations toward closer "nonalignment" with the socialist bloc. Although U.S. policymakers could (and did) disagree about the extent of the Cuban threat and how best to contain it, there was no mistaking the principal source of Washington's concern over Cuba.[4]

With the collapse of the Soviet Union, however, Cuba's threat to U.S. security—or at least traditional conceptions of it—was rendered moot. Without Soviet support, Cuba could no longer project military power far from its shores. In need of new trade partners to replace its former allies, Cuba could no longer afford to antagonize its Latin American neighbors by fomenting revolution. Indeed, what Cuba needed more than anything was to find some way of coexisting with former adversaries, Washington included, in order to ease the island's economic recovery.

Despite Washington's triumph in the international system and the evaporation of the Cuban threat, U.S. policy has remained one of hostility, isolation, and economic denial. In fact, U.S. sanctions have gotten tougher as the Cuban threat has waned. As Susan Kaufman Purcell details in Chapter 5, the Cuban Democracy Act of 1992 (commonly referred to as the Torricelli bill) and the Cuban Liberty and Democratic Solidarity (Libertad) Act of 1996 (known as the Helms-Burton bill) both tightened economic sanctions against Cuba and raised the threshold for lifting them. When Presidents Gerald Ford and Jimmy Carter initiated their ill-fated efforts to normalize relations with Cuba in the 1970s, the quid pro quo they demanded was a less aggressive Cuban foreign policy in Africa and Latin America. Today, nothing short of the demise of the current Cuban regime will suffice. Helms-Burton freezes U.S. policy until both Fidel Castro and his brother Raúl have departed the scene and a new democratic government takes over that is willing to pay compensation to Cuban Americans whose property was nationalized in the 1960s.

David J. Rothkopf argues that this shift in the U.S. agenda contravenes the national interest. A debate over Cuba should begin, he contends, by asking what is at stake for the United States. He sees only two compelling interests: the danger of uncontrolled migration (as happened during the 1980 Mariel crisis and the 1994 rafters' crisis); and the potential for Cuba to become a staging area (with or without government complicity) for narcotics trafficking and terrorism. Ironically, both these threats are intensified by U.S. policies that seek to weaken the Cuban economy and undermine its government. Weakening the economy intensifies migration pressures, and weakening the government diminishes its ability to combat international crime and impedes bilateral cooperation on law enforcement. Current U.S. policy also entails tangential costs, Rothkopf contends: it irritates our allies (because of the extraterritorial pretensions of Helms-Burton), blocks U.S. businesspeople from opportunities in Cuba, and plays directly into Castro's propensity to blame adversity on the United States.

In reply to the argument that Washington has a responsibility to promote democracy in Cuba, Rothkopf responds with the realist's observation that we do business with undemocratic regimes all the time. Promoting democracy is a worthy goal, but it is neither the only nor even the highest foreign policy priority—nor should it be. In this regard Cuba ought to be treated no differently than any other country.

Rothkopf's remedy is to normalize relations. Washington should lift economic sanctions and pursue a policy of dialogue and engagement. Perhaps engagement will have the salutary impact of speeding reform in Cuba, Rothkopf surmises, but he wisely notes that no U.S. policy is likely to have a decisive impact on Cuban government policy. Rather, his main argument is that lifting sanctions will ease Cuba's economic pain, thereby reducing the danger of a "social meltdown" that could unleash real threats to U.S. national interests. In short, while he would prefer to see Cuba evolve toward democracy, Rothkopf concludes that a stable Cuba, even an undemocratic one, is less of a threat to U.S. interests than instability.

Susan Kaufman Purcell disagrees. She defends recent U.S. policy as an increasingly sophisticated effort to maintain pressure on the Cuban government, thereby speeding its demise, while at the same time engaging the Cuban people. She is not distressed that promoting democracy has replaced U.S. security as the predominant concern of U.S. policy toward Cuba. Since the fall of communism, this essentially Wilsonian imperative has grown increasingly prominent in U.S. foreign policy, especially in cases (like Cuba) where residual security concerns are slight and business opportunities limited. But Purcell's main argument in favor of hanging tough is pragmatic: engagement, as practiced by Canada and Western Europe, has been singularly ineffective in promoting any political opening. This is a deft reply to the perennial criticism of the U.S. embargo: after forty years, the embargo has failed either to oust Fidel Castro or to extract significant concessions from him. Purcell is right to note that engagement's track record, albeit of shorter duration, is no better.

Purcell's argument in favor of U.S. economic sanctions is straight-forward. Lifting the embargo would inevitably facilitate resource transfers to Cuba (from U.S. tourists and businesspeople) that would accrue primarily to the government, thereby strengthening it. Strengthening the Cuban government will only delay the transition to a more open economy and polity, because Fidel Castro is hostile to both, and he will avoid them if at all possible. The market-oriented economic reforms introduced in the 1990s were forced and grudging, and are likely to be reversed at the first opportunity. Easing the government's plight would only hasten this retreat, whereas maintaining economic pressure may hasten a regime transition.

In fact, arguing for the efficacy of U.S. sanctions, Purcell claims that the pain inflicted by the Torricelli and Helms-Burton bills can be credited with forcing economic reform on the Cuban government. Andrew Zimbalist's chapter on the Cuban economy does not go as far, making the case that Cuba's crisis stemmed directly from the loss of Soviet subsidies, next to which the incremental economic damage inflicted by Washington pales in comparison. But the central logic of Purcell's argument does not depend on U.S. sanctions forcing economic reforms on Castro; it rests instead on the more plausible claim that denying resources to Cuba is more likely to shorten Castro's tenure than to extend it.

As an alternative to improving state-to-state relations between the United States and Cuba, Purcell endorses the idea of expanding people-to-people contacts, including the transfer of resources. She sees this as a way of easing the burdens of the economic crisis on ordinary Cubans, thereby defusing the principal humanitarian argument against economic embargoes—that they hurt poor people while leaving the elite unscathed. Moreover, by encouraging people-to-people contacts, the United States might strengthen Cuban civil society, diminish Castro's ability to rally Cuban nationalism against the Colossus of the North, and thereby set the stage for better relations in the post-Castro era.

It is hard to argue against people-to-people contact; only the most dogmatic hard-liners (on both sides of the straits) are willing to forgo its humanitarian benefits in order to maintain ideological purity. There are, however, inherent limits to expanding people-to-people contacts in a context of state-to-state hostility. Conservative Cuban Americans rightly argue that any resource transfers to the island, even family remittances, are partially appropriated by the government, thereby strengthening it economically. The sharp analytical line Purcell draws between denial of resources to the Cuban government and engaging the Cuban people is much less clear in practice. Implicitly, there is a trade-off: engaging the Cuban people may strengthen the economy, thereby easing pressure on the government. This is by no means hypothetical; remittances flowing into Cuba are estimated at between U.S.$600 million and $800 million annually.

Across the straits, Cuban officials, especially those responsible for state security, regard U.S. efforts to engage and promote nongovernmental groups on the island as intentionally subversive. It does not help that U.S. officials occasionally describe such activity in precisely those terms. U.S. efforts to revitalize Cuban civil society may have the opposite effect if the efforts enable the Cuban government to brand non-governmental groups as tools (witting or unwitting) of a foreign enemy. Labeling internal opponents as agents of the United States has long been Fidel Castro's trump card. No doubt he will continue to use it regardless, but Washington should not make it any easier for him.

Despite their diametrically opposed prescriptions for U.S. policy, Rothkopf and Purcell profess to seek the same end: a process of peaceful change in Cuba that avoids widespread violence. For Rothkopf, avoiding violence has top priority, and by his own admission, engagement may not contribute much to the process of change. For Purcell, promoting change is more important, even if a policy of hostility is more likely to result in change that is apocalyptic rather than peaceful.

Apart from the relative merits of these policy alternatives, the politics of the issue clearly favors continued U.S. hostility. In the past two decades, the Cuban American community, especially its well-organized and well-funded conservative wing, has become the dominant influence over U.S. policy, playing a critical role in the passage of both the Torricelli and Helms-Burton bills. There is a diversity of views among Cuban Americans, to be sure, especially among the younger generation born in the United States. On humanitarian issues (the expansion of communications, travel, humanitarian aid, and remittances), most Cuban Americans favor increased contact with the island, conservative hard-liners notwithstanding. Nevertheless, the overwhelming majority of Cuban Americans are still viscerally hostile to the Castro regime and would vehemently oppose a normalization of U.S.-Cuban relations.[5]

Organized, single-minded, and geographically concentrated in the key electoral states of Florida and New Jersey, Cuban Americans can inflict severe political pain on any public official who even hints at rapprochement with Castro. There is no countervailing constituency. The

U.S. business community would like to have access to Cuba and has been more vocal recently in calling for a change in policy. But the Cuban market is small, Cuba is poor, and the near-term business opportunities are limited. The lobbying arms of major corporations have more pressing concerns than Cuba. The general public cares not at all about Cuba, except during waves of uncontrolled immigration from the island.

Rothkopf contends that with the demise of the Cuban security threat, Cuba policy, for all intents and purposes, has ceased to be a foreign policy issue, becoming instead a highly symbolic domestic political issue.[6] He accuses politicians of pandering to the Cuban American community, but identifies no strategy for circumventing the community's potent opposition to any change in policy. Since Purcell's policy preferences coincide with those of the community, she is less disturbed by its influence, but she acknowledges that a change in U.S. policy is highly unlikely in the face of Cuban American opposition. It may well be that the normalization of U.S. relations with Cuba must await the passing of both the generation that made the revolution of 1959 and the generation that fled from it.

All the chapters in this volume reverberate with the shock that Cuba has suffered in the decade since the collapse of the Soviet Union. The authors, like the Cubans themselves, are trying to comprehend the magnitude of the changes that have been set in motion and to predict the trajectory of the Cuban economy and polity. In times of rapid and unprecedented change, no prediction is likely to be completely correct, but the authors do a laudable job of laying out the topography and scouting possible paths forward. Even in their disagreements, they show the reader which features of the landscape are least clear and why. Together, they provide an invaluable picture of how things stand in Cuba today and the shape of things to come.

Notes

1. See, for example, John Plank, ed., *Cuba and the United States: Long Range Perspectives* (Washington, DC: Brookings Institution, 1967).

2. See Castro's speech to the Cuban National Assembly, December 28, 1993, quoted in Ana Julia Jatar-Hausmann, *The Cuban Way: Capitalism, Communism, and Confrontation* (West Hartford, CT: Kumarian Press, 1999), p. 53.

3. In 1996, Raúl Castro denounced certain party-connected think tanks for having developed relations with foreigners that were too cozy and hence ideologically contaminated. His speech, a report from the Political Bureau to the Central Committee of the Communist Party, is in "The Political and Social Situation in Cuba and the Corresponding Tasks of the Party," *Granma International* (April 1996).

4. For a good discussion of the role security concerns have played in U.S. policy toward Cuba both during and after the Cold War, see Jorge I. Domínguez, "U.S.–Latin American Relations During the Cold War and Its Aftermath," in *The United States and Latin America: The New Agenda,* eds. Victor Bulmer-Thomas and James Dunkerley (Cambridge, MA: Harvard University Press, 1999), pp. 33–50.

5. For a thorough recent study of the Cuban American community, see Maxine Molyneux, "The Politics of the Cuban Diaspora in the United States," in *The United States and Latin America: The New Agenda*, eds. Victor Bulmer-Thomas and James Dunkerley (Cambridge, MA: Harvard University Press, 1999), pp. 287–310.

6. I have argued as much myself, in William M. LeoGrande, "From Havana to Miami: U.S. Cuba Policy as a Two-Level Game," *Journal of Interamerican Studies and World Affairs* 40, no. 1 (spring 1998): 67–86.

2

Whither the Cuban Economy?

Andrew Zimbalist

The Cuban revolution has made enormous strides since 1959 in providing basic social services to all its citizens and in establishing certain norms of equity and equality. Free, universally available public education and medical care rank at the top of these achievements. The economic crisis of the past decade, however, has meant that Cuba's social safety net is increasingly tattered. It is even more striking that the society's norms of equity and equality have been thoroughly undermined. One recent study found that the share of income going to the top 5 percent of Cubans rose from 10.1 percent in 1986 to 31.0 percent in 1995. Cuba has become a class society, defined by access to hard currency through work, politics, or family abroad. Material rewards in Cuba today do not correspond in any meaningful way with one's economic contribution. Racial disparities and tensions have also grown, as Cuban blacks, who had benefited tremendously from the revolution, were hit hard by the economic collapse. The economic situation of blacks has been exacerbated by the fact that they have been less likely to emigrate than whites and, thus, have fewer relatives abroad to provide them with hard currency.

Universal education and health care, albeit diminished in quality, are still important institutions in Cuban society, as are production cooperatives in agriculture and a large state sector in industry. The best guarantee of the longevity of these institutions is to situate them within a viable development context and model. Cuba's present

13

model is simply no longer viable. The longer it is rigidly pursued, the more likely it is that the present system will come to a violent and destructive end. The more flexibly and rapidly it is reformed, the more likely it is that Cuba will be able to make a peaceful and successful transition to a mixed economy, one rooted in the market but offering its citizens a strong social safety net.

The Cuban economy experienced a massive external shock with the dissolution of the Soviet trading bloc during 1989–1991. In response, the economy began to decentralize. Cuba's precipitous economic decline was arrested, but the process of substantial structural reform was essentially halted in 1994. Today, Cuba is left with a limping economy in limbo. Although the government has made serious efforts to maintain its social safety net—increasing spending on social assistance in 1998 by 32.6 percent, on housing and community services by 16.8 percent, and on public health by 7.1 percent[1]— the severity of the nation's economic problems makes it difficult to reverse the decline in the standard of living. According to official Cuban statistics, if Cuba maintains its 1994–1998 annual rate of real per capita GDP growth of 2.3 percent, the Cuban people will not enjoy their 1991 level of per capita income again until the year 2009.

Cuba's Current Economic Reality

Analyzing the Cuban economy is not an easy task. The Cuban government has made only limited information available to the public since 1989. In 1994, it published an eleven-page booklet entitled *La Economía Cubana,* the Central Bank issues periodic *Informes,* and government officials occasionally cite statistics in their public speeches or interviews. This opaqueness was diminished significantly in August 1997 when the United Nations' Economic Commission for Latin America and the Caribbean (CEPAL) published a major study on the Cuban economy, complete with a statistical appendix.[2] While this study was a welcome contribution, it was based largely on data provided by the Cuban government and was not nearly as comprehensive as the *Anuarios Estadísticos* of the 1980s. Further, the CEPAL study contained many internal inconsistencies and, most troubling of all, did not explain the methodological practices and assumptions underlying the data. Thus, the would-be analyst must still engage in substantial detective work to understand the Cuban economy, as the following example suggests.

In the 1994 *Informe* the government published aggregate macro-economic data—the first since 1989—suggesting that Cuba's GDP increased by 0.7 percent in 1994. This figure needs to be taken with a grain of salt. The government does not explain its methodology in shifting to the Western system of national accounts from the previous Soviet accounting system—a move made in the early nineties. There is no explanation, among other things, about sectoral weights, the treatment of prices, or how the government accounts, if at all, for informal economic activity. Consider, for instance, government reports that during the fourth quarter of 1994 there were 470 million pesos of food sold at the new farmers' markets. Since a similar quantity of food was probably produced and sold on the black market in 1993 and, thus, was not counted in GDP, the legalization of the farmers' markets alone would raise the official GDP figure by approximately 470 million pesos. That is, measured GDP rose, even though actual production did not. If we adjust for this, GDP would have fallen in 1994 by 3.7 percent, rather than grown by 0.7 percent. On the other hand, growth in the informal market during 1994 was robust and most of it was probably not recorded. Hence, on balance, it is possible that the level of economic activity was similar to the government estimate.

The turnaround in growth reflected in the official statistics for 1994 continued during 1995–1998, with reported economic growth of 2.5 percent in 1995, a reported 7.8 percent in 1996, 2.5 percent in 1997, and 1.2 percent in 1998 (see Table 2.1).[3] With the rapid growth of legalized hard-currency markets, however, there is a substantial question about the extent to which this recorded growth simply reflects transactions that had previously been underground and were not counted. In any event, the rapid growth of 1996 has not been sustained, and the prospects are not good that it will resume on a steady basis anytime in the near future.

The basic outline of Cuba's economic predicament is clear. In 1988–1989, Cuba received 85 percent of its imports and several billion dollars in subsidies from the Soviet bloc. In addition, Cuba received 12–13 million tons of oil from the former Soviet Union. By 1994, imports of Russian oil had fallen below 2 million tons, Cuba's

Table 2.1 **Real Annual GDP Growth Rates in Cuba, 1991–1998**
(official statistics)

	1991	1992	1993	1994	1995	1996	1997	1998	1991– 1998	1994– 1998
GDP (%)	−10.9	−11.2	−14.7	0.6	2.4	7.8	2.5	1.2	−2.55	2.87
Population (%)	0.7	0.6	0.5	0.6	0.6	0.5	0.5	0.4	0.57	0.53
GDP per capita (%)	−11.6	−11.8	−15.2	0.0	1.8	7.3	2.0	0.8	−3.12	2.34

Sources: CEPAL, *Balance Preliminar de las Economías de América Latina y el Caribe, 1998*, pp. 88–89; José Luis Rodríguez, *Intervención ante la Asamblea Nacional del Poder Popular*, December 21, 1998.

total goods imports had dropped from U.S.$8.1 billion in 1989 to under $2.0 billion in 1994, and all sources of Soviet aid had dried up.

Unlike 1959–1960, when U.S. trade with Cuba evaporated and the Soviet Union was there to bail Cuba out, no one has been willing to play this role in the post-1990 period. Indeed, under pressure from an ardent, well-organized, deep-pocketed, and conservative Cuban American lobby, the United States has only moved to tighten its embargo, which the Cubans estimate to have cost them over U.S.$60 billion to date, with annual costs near $1 billion in recent years.

A vicious cycle set in. Without foreign exchange, output fell rapidly and shortages became ubiquitous. The government response was to give priority to the maintenance of basic social services and near-full employment. This policy, while helping to prevent the potentially devastating social consequences of shock economic policies, led to a 90 percent increase in the government budget deficit, which reached 5.05 billion pesos in 1993.

If Cuba had an independent central bank and a bond market, the government would finance its deficits by selling bonds to the public. Although this could have inflationary implications under certain circumstances, there would be no direct connection to excess liquidity. (Liquidity refers to the amount of assets that are available to use for the purchase of goods and services. Most frequently, it refers to funds in checking accounts and cash in the hands of the public.) In the absence of an independent central bank and a bond market, such deficits in Cuba have traditionally been financed directly through printing money, leading to a growing problem of excess liquidity. Indeed, by the end of 1993, the Cuban economy had an accumulated liquidity of 11.04 billion pesos, more than three times as large as the Cuban government itself estimated as desirable at that time. The excess money supply was compounded by a growing shortage of goods engendered by the precipitous drop in Cuban imports and the tightening of the U.S. embargo. Thus, the Cuban money supply increased from 23.9 percent of GDP in 1990 to 66.5 percent in 1993.[4] Simply put, there was too much money chasing too few goods, and Cuban workers were increasingly being paid in pesos that they could not spend. Workers lost any monetary incentive to work, a development exacerbated by the growing difficulty in getting to work via a nearly dysfunctional public-transportation system and the absence of necessary raw materials and spare parts at their workplaces. A black market developed in which prices, due to pent-up demand, were out of the reach of most budgets. Workers in the state sector connived to divert raw materials and goods to the black market, further undermining the state sector's capacity to produce.

Not only was finance from the former Soviet trade bloc cut off, but Cuba had stopped paying its medium- and long-term hard-currency debt in the mid-1980s, making it impossible for Cuba to obtain anything but begrudging and expensive short-term trade financing. (Virtually all foreign trade must be financed, that is, bank credits must be available in order for the producer to be paid in local currency before the good is delivered.) Under these circumstances, Cuba turned to foreign capital to establish tourist and export enclaves—sectors that are largely detached from the rest of the economy and that focus their production on the export market. Here some gains were made in attracting foreign capital, but the flow of foreign investment was too slow and too small to make much of a dent in Cuba's economic free fall. By the end of 1993, according to official Cuban statistics, the Cuban economy was producing approximately 35 percent less than it had in 1989, or roughly 40 percent less in per capita terms.

The Cuban government had little choice but to take some significant reform measures. A four-part program was initiated in 1994 with the goal of gradually reducing the excess liquidity in the economy. Measures included price increases for several consumer goods and services; the abolition of certain free services; the introduction of new taxes; and the reduction of subsidies to state enterprises, most of which run a deficit. These policies, along with increased sales of cigars and alcoholic beverages to the Cuban public, resulted in some modest initial success, reducing excess liquidity by around 25 percent by mid-1995.

These fiscal reforms were accompanied by several important structural changes. In July 1993, the government made it legal for Cubans to use U.S. dollars. Dollars were already used widely in the informal economy. By legalizing their use, the government hoped to bring these dollars out of the underground economy and into open trade activity where they could be captured by the government.[5] Other measures included the expansion of self-employment opportunities and the cooperativization of most state farms beginning in September 1993;[6] reopening of the farmers' markets in October 1994;[7] introduction of industrial and craft markets in December 1994; and the opening in mid-1995 of hard-currency exchanges called CADECAs, where Cubans can exchange pesos for dollars or vice versa. Each of these reforms represented a small step toward promoting decentralization, individual initiative, market incentives, and greater efficiency.

The fiscal and structural reforms, together with an inflow of several hundred million dollars in foreign investment and growing remittances from Cuban exiles,[8] were sufficient to thwart the economic downfall and initiate a mild recovery. During 1994–1998, the Cuban economy experienced a real annual growth rate of 2.9 percent, or 2.3 percent in per capita terms—a rate not far below the 3.6 percent per capita growth experienced by the rest of Latin America and the Caribbean over the same period. Let us take a closer look.

Three Distinct Economies

Cuba today has three distinct economies. First, there is the traditional public sector characterized by state ownership, fixed prices, and central administration. This sector still accounts for more than three-quarters of the official labor force. At least 200,000 workers have been laid off from jobs in the public sector over the past four years. To be sure, this is a large number of layoffs, but capacity utilization in the state sector is still only around 35 percent due to a shortage of inputs and lack of demand.[9] CEPAL estimates that the government would need to lay off another 400,000 or more workers to put these enterprises on a competitive basis in terms of productivity.[10]

Second, there is the export enclave sector characterized by state and joint state-foreign ownership and a reliance on foreign technology, capital, management, and marketing skills. This sector, which caters to the international market, encompasses tourism, nickel, tobacco, citrus, fishing, and biotechnology. With the exception of biotechnology, which has held steady, each of these sectors is experiencing modest to good growth.

Third, there is the informal and market sector, made up of self-employment, production above state quotas, production destined for the export sector, hard-currency shops, farmers' markets, industrial and craft markets, and black markets. These markets in general have been dynamic. For example, in 1996, Cubans spent $627 million in hard-currency shops, 18 percent more than in 1995. At the parallel-market rate of exchange, this amount equaled approximately 13.8 billion pesos, or 54.8 percent of official current-price GDP (25.2 billion pesos).[11] Hard-currency shop sales grew another 17.8 percent in 1997 and 15 percent in 1998.[12] In 1996, Cuban families spent at least two-thirds of their budget on informal and free markets, and there is no reason to expect that this proportion fell in subsequent years.

The growing importance of hard currency within the Cuban economy has obligated the Cuban government and foreign companies operating on the island to use hard-currency bonuses to motivate their workers.[13] In March 1998, 1.5 million workers received hard-currency incentives or payments in kind averaging $53 each per year, an amount equivalent to more than five months of average wages in parallel-market pesos. In Cuba's perverse economic environment, these hard-currency rewards are useful in mitigating the distorted incentives that enable hotel chambermaids, bellhops, taxi drivers, prostitutes, and others working in the dollar-based economy to earn several times more than engineers, doctors, or manufacturing workers. Unfortunately, while reducing the distortion, the hard-currency bonuses are not sufficiently large to reverse the trend of doctors becoming cabbies or lawyers moving into retailing, or to create an incentive for students to stay in school to increase their human capital. Nor will hard-currency bonuses diminish the pervasive rent-seeking behavior practiced throughout the Cuban economy. (Rent-seeking refers to the ability of a person or corporation to benefit because of a political appointment or role in a monopolized market. An example of rent-seeking behavior in Cuba is when buyers for state companies demand a 3 percent commission from a foreign company before signing an import contract. While the individual gains, society loses, as prices become less efficient.)

Fiscal and Monetary Imbalance

The Cuban government has made significant strides toward fiscal and monetary balance. Fiscal balance generally refers to a balanced budget and monetary situation where, given the institutions and practices of the financial system, the population is holding neither too much nor too little money to purchase the goods being produced. Monetary balance is necessary if Cuba is to restore the peso as the economy's currency. Although the central-budget deficit, after growing to 30.4 percent of GDP in 1993, was reduced to just over 2 percent of GDP in 1997, and the money supply has been cut by some 25 percent, these figures understate the extent of the problem. First, CEPAL suggests that a significant part of the deficit reduction is due, on the one hand, to substituting central-bank loans and growing accounts receivable for budget subsidies to state enterprises and, on the other hand, to shifting some central expenditures to local governments.[14]

Second, some imbalances are still huge. Whereas the Cuban government has estimated that the appropriate level of liquidity for the economy is 3.5 billion pesos, liquidity at the end of 1998 was 9.46 billion pesos, or over 2.5 times its desired level. In reality, matters are even worse: with hundreds of millions of dollars circulating in Cuba, at the parallel-market rate of exchange the total liquidity represented by the dollar is 130 percent that of the peso. Further, the trade deficit is large and growing, rising from $0.5 billion in 1995, to $1.08 billion in 1996, to $1.95 billion in 1997, or well over half of Cuba's total exports. In 1998, Cuba's current account balance—the value of exports of all goods and services, minus the value of imports of all goods and services—grew to over $300 million,[15] while Cuba's budget deficit increased to 2.5 percent of GDP. According to the economic plan for 1999, the budget deficit is projected to reach 3 percent of GDP.[16]

It is clear that Cuba needs to push forward more aggressively in its pursuit of economic balance. Further reductions in the government deficit are necessary, but they will entail massive layoffs of state-sector workers. The only way to cushion this blow socially is through the expansion of other sectors. For other sectors to expand, in turn, there must be new investment, which brings us to another salient feature of the Cuban economy today—a lack of investment.

Lack of Investment

The ratio of investment to GDP in Cuba, which stood at 24.3 percent in 1989 and 21 percent in 1991, fell to an average of 6.3 percent during 1994–1996. Since GDP was lower during 1994–1996 than in 1989, the absolute drop in investment spending is even greater than these proportions suggest, probably in the neighborhood of 80–85 percent.

All machinery and equipment wears down, or depreciates, over time. A country's capital stock—the value of its machinery, equipment, and infrastructure—will grow only if the new investments in a particular year exceed the amount of depreciation in its existing capital stock. It is reasonable to expect that depreciation in Cuba today is in the neighborhood of 8 to 14 percent of GDP; hence, at the 1994–1996 investment rate Cuba is actually being decapitalized. This situation obviously will not allow for long-term growth. Cuba must increase its capital stock if it hopes to sustain economic growth.

Cuba's capital shortage is even more severe than these numbers suggest because of the nation's increasing demographic maturity. In 1960, 8 percent of the population was over sixty years of age; in 1990, 12 percent of the population was over sixty; and, by 2015, due to low birth rates and growing longevity, 18 percent of the population is projected to be over sixty. Since individuals over sixty tend to have negative savings, this will create a downward bias in the savings rate for Cuba and capital formation will become even more difficult.

Consider Cuba's recent investment experience. With few exceptions, there has been no appreciable investment in the traditional state sector, which includes almost all industrial, mining, transport, military, and utility production, along with state farms, most tourism and finance, and a substantial share of other services. The state's precarious fiscal situation makes it unlikely that this condition will change much in the coming years. The other two possible arenas for investment are the informal sector and foreign investment. Let us look at each in turn.

While private activity in the informal sector flourished until 1998, it has since been tightly circumscribed by government policies that basically forbid capital accumulation in this sphere. Consider, for instance, the treatment of *paladares* (private, family-run restaurants). First, as is true throughout Cuba's private sector (apart from a few puzzling exceptions), the *paladares* are not allowed to hire outside labor. The proscription on hiring "wage labor" is common to all socialist economies and derives from Marxist notions of exploitation. More practically, the Cuban government limits the hiring of outside labor because it fears the consequent growth of a powerful private sector. Second, the owners of the *paladares* must provide government agents with receipts proving that they obtained all their food through legal channels. Third, they must pay a monthly license fee of $375, plus 1,500 Cuban pesos to the government.

Fourth, private restaurant owners pay a progressive income tax with top rates at 50 percent on all revenues after deducting 10 percent for costs, making the tax rates on actual net income confiscatory. For instance, suppose there is a *paladar* with revenues of 1,000 pesos and actual costs of 500 pesos. According to the government tax policy, this *paladar* would be allowed to deduct only 10 percent of its revenues, or 100 pesos, as its costs, and would have to pay a 50 percent tax on 900 pesos (1,000 pesos of revenue minus 100 pesos of reportable costs). Thus, the tax would be 450 pesos on an actual net income of 500 pesos (1,000 pesos of revenue minus 500 pesos of actual costs). This amounts to an effective tax rate of 90 percent. Fifth, restaurants are limited to twelve seats and may only serve seated customers. Take-out customers are not permitted. It was no surprise, then, when the government reported that retail food sales fell 14.7 percent in 1998.[17]

Under conditions such as these, it is hard to imagine any capital accumulation occurring in the private sector. The few private operators who manage to accumulate significant after-tax income generally find ways to transfer their capital outside Cuba, since accumulation inside the country is permitted only in low-yielding savings accounts.

By December 1995, officially sanctioned self-employment had reached over 200,000, but many operators have since gone underground to avoid onerous state taxes and regulations, while others have been closed down by the government. By late 1998, the number of self-employed was below 160,000.[18] This is especially problematic because the private service sector is labor-intensive and would provide an excellent arena to absorb the half million or more excess workers in state enterprises.

Existing controls spawn under-the-table payoffs to government monitors and encourage black-market transactions. Regulations here need to be liberalized and wholesale markets legalized and allowed to flourish.

Foreign Investment

Cuba has benefited significantly from the foreign investment that has occurred to date. These inflows have provided the catalyst for much of the productive activity in the present economy, namely, the rejuvenation in agriculture and industry to supply the bustling tourist and hard-currency markets. Foreign investment has also been a catalyst in transforming Cuba's business culture from one rooted in the complacency and waste of central planning toward one based on competition and market efficiency.

The flow of foreign investment appears to have slowed significantly in recent years. Most outside observers estimate that total foreign-investment disbursements in Cuba amount to approximately $1 billion, a figure that stands in sharp contrast to the official figure of $2 billion-plus provided by government officials.[19] One explanation of the disparity is that the official figure seems to include investments that have been committed but not yet disbursed. A recent Economist Intelligence Unit report on the Cuban economy, for instance, reports modest foreign-direct-investment flows of $563 million in 1994, $5 million in 1995, and $80 million in 1996.[20]

In March 1996, the U.S. Congress passed the Helms-Burton bill, which was designed to further tighten the U.S. embargo by punishing foreign companies (and their executives) that "traffic" in expropriated U.S. property in Cuba. One of the intentions of the law was to curb the flow of foreign investment into Cuba. While several new investment accords have been signed since the passage of Helms-Burton, most of these have been for small investments and to some degree they have been offset by canceled projects. Sherritt, a Canadian company with investments in several sectors of the Cuban economy, raised some $600 million in Canadian capital markets to invest in Cuba, but little new investment has materialized. Apart from some tourism projects, a cellular-phone investment projected at around $35 million (which does not represent new capital for Cuba

since Sherritt is buying out a Mexican investor), an $18 million in-
vestment in soybean processing, and another modest investment in
secondary natural-gas recovery employing Japanese turbines, Sherritt has not been able to find suitable places to invest the funds it has
raised. Similar problems have been reported for other Cuban investment funds.

In his speech before the National Assembly of Popular Power in
December 1998, Carlos Lage, a leading member of the politburo and
chief adviser to Castro on economic affairs, affirmed the difficulties
Cuba is having in attracting foreign capital, even to the tourism sector: "Until now foreign investment [in tourism] has been very reduced, coming via management contracts and the remodeling of
some of the hotels where there are management contracts."[21] Cuba's
inability to attract more foreign investment is particularly troubling
given its rapid increase throughout Latin America, where yearly foreign investment rose from $8.4 billion in 1990, to $30.2 billion in
1994, to $50 billion in 1997. Considering the Caribbean alone, for-
eign investment in 1997 grew by 25 percent to $4.5 billion.

The problem in part is Helms-Burton, in part Cuba's labor costs
and government-controlled labor market for foreign companies, and
in part other factors. Another issue for Cuba is the tendency for foreign investment to concentrate in natural resource–intensive sectors
(for example, tourism and agriculture) and energy-intensive sectors
(such as nickel). With a shortage of energy but an abundance of
highly educated labor, Cuba's long-term development needs seem to
require investment in certain technology-intensive sectors—areas
where Cuba had been developing a specialization before the collapse
of the Soviet trading bloc.

In June 1996, Cuba passed legislation to open free-trade zones
(FTZs) with the hope of attracting new foreign investments in light-
assembly operations and warehousing. The first was opened in 1997;
currently there are four. Three are managed by *Almacenes Unidas,*
a company under the control of the Armed Forces, and the fourth is
managed by Cimex, a joint venture controlled by the Cuban government. Compared to other zones in the Caribbean, FTZ legislation in
Cuba tends to be highly favorable to foreign companies. For instance, foreign companies operating in Cuba's FTZs can sell their
products to the Cuban market without duty if local value added is 50
percent or more. In spite of generally favorable terms, as of February 1998, Cuba's FTZs had attracted only one small manufacturer,
a Jamaican company that produces powdered mixes for soft drinks

and employs about forty Cuban workers. The company is allowed to sell only to the Cuban market in its first two years of operation, at which point it must begin exporting.

There are two main problems with Cuba's FTZs. First, the U.S. embargo makes warehousing and processing of goods in Cuba ill-advised since such goods cannot enter the United States, the hemisphere's largest market and the one closest to Cuba. Also, the Dominican Republic and other Caribbean countries have abundant FTZs that are not affected by the embargo. Second, companies operating in Cuba's FTZs are treated in the same way as all foreign investors on the island in that they must hire their workers indirectly through government agencies and pay the agencies in dollars at the official peso/dollar exchange rate. The agencies, in turn, pay the workers in pesos according to the prevailing wage scale in Cuba. This system has significant disadvantages for the foreign company. The company does not have direct control over its labor force and sometimes is compelled to hire workers who have been selected by the government agency based on their political loyalty rather than their productivity. In addition, labor costs in Cuba are higher than elsewhere in the region. The average compensation (wage plus benefits) for a Cuban worker in the FTZ is approximately $1.50/hour, not including in-kind payments to the workforce. In contrast, compensation in the Dominican Republic's FTZs is closer to $1.00/hour.[22] With substantially higher compensation, it is not surprising that Cuba has failed to attract export-oriented companies to its FTZs.

For all these reasons, it is difficult to conclude that under current circumstances Cuba can rely on foreign investment to generate the capital accumulation needed for sustained economic growth. Real interest rates on household savings in pesos have been negative. A growing share of the population (56.3 percent in 1998, according to official figures) holds hard currency, and these savings do have a positive real yield. However, prevented from growing their own enterprises or investing in other productive activity, Cubans ultimately find themselves obliged to spend their hard currency on consumption. Thus, the present model, with insufficient investment in the state and foreign sectors and virtually no investment in the private sphere, does not offer a viable basis for short-term economic balancing or for longer-term economic growth.

Such growth is needed not only to support fiscal balancing, but also to cushion the necessary layoffs of half a million or more workers in the public sector (CEPAL estimates that unemployment and underemployment in Cuba is at 34.1 percent)[23] and to raise incomes. The average real wage in Cuba fell by approximately 40 percent between 1989 and 1995, using the official GDP deflator—an indicator that reveals how rapidly prices in the entire economy are rising. If black-market prices and the fast-growing share of purchases that occur on informal and free markets are also considered, the real wage would have fallen by considerably more. For instance, CEPAL estimates that the price of a basket of ninety-one basic goods increased 660 percent between 1989 and 1995, suggesting that real wages fell by over 80 percent.

Conclusion

The main engine for incentives, productivity, and potential growth in Cuba today is the market. Central planning and state resource allocation served a useful developmental function in promoting early industrialization in Cuba, and arguably remained viable as long as Cuba was able to concentrate its trade within the Soviet bloc. But Cuba's economy is considerably more complex today than it was in 1960 and is no longer sheltered by a trading bloc of planned economies. Cuba is far too small to contemplate development without an open economy. Cuba will only succeed in the world economy if competitive forces are allowed to influence resource allocation and motivate producers.

There is no reason the government cannot modify the market-determined allocation of resources via supply management mechanisms in order to create comparative advantages in certain sectors. (A comparative advantage exists when a country is relatively more efficient than other countries in producing certain goods, even if in absolute terms it is less efficient at producing all goods.) Nor is there any reason a significant part of Cuban industry cannot remain in state hands.

To the extent that state enterprises are to play a role, however, they will do it better if they are fewer and if they face competition from a vibrant private sector. Cuba has shown a willingness to admit the market into sectors of its economy, but it has also closely regulated and circumscribed its penetration. Cuban officials need to look more seriously at a mixed economy, and consider introducing into the industrial sphere ownership reforms similar to those that have already been carried out in agriculture. In this sector, approximately 15 percent of the arable land is owned by private individual farmers, 52 percent is operated by private cooperatives, and only 33 percent is owned and operated by the state (although the private sector in agriculture is still closely regulated).

Cooperativization and privatization of sectors of industry would have several potentially salutary side effects. Such changes would decentralize management and provide workers with more direct incentives to improve efficiency and raise output. They would provide the state with a source of revenue from selling off its assets, thereby promoting a quicker monetary balance. They would create an ownership class of Cubans who have been living on the island throughout the revolution, rather than encouraging the present dichotomy in which foreigners (including Cuban exiles) are allowed to own productive assets and employ workers while resident Cubans are not. Furthermore, these changes would allow such a class to be established before Cuban exiles return to the island to buy up productive assets after the U.S. embargo is lifted. If such a reform is not implemented, the Cuban economy will one day be owned largely by those who lived in exile during the revolution. While the Cuban government is not anxious to establish a private ownership class today, it should be concerned that those who remained in Cuba will be without substantial productive holdings in a capitalist Cuba of the future.

Such measures certainly depart from socialist orthodoxy in Cuba. However, the vision of society that optimists believed was supported by this orthodoxy is now shattered and cannot be recovered. More practical policies are needed to salvage the revolution's social gains and to avert the possibility of an abrupt, violent, and devastating collapse of the present system.

Notes

1. See CEPAL, *Balance Preliminar de las Economías de América Latina y el Caribe, 1999,* pp. 77–79, and the speeches by José Luis Rodríguez, Osvaldo Martínez, and Carlos Lage before the National Assembly of Popular Power on December 21, 1998.

2. CEPAL, *La Economía Cubana: Reformas Estructurales y Desempeño en los Noventa* (Mexico City, August 1997).

3. Lower sugar and nickel prices hurt Cuban exports in 1998, but lower petroleum import prices more than made up for their negative current-account effect. Sugar output in 1998 fell 24 percent from its already low level in 1997 to 3.2 million tons. According to Carlos Lage, speech, op. cit., Cuban GDP would have risen by 4.1 percent in 1998 if the sugar sector had been excluded.

4. See Ana Julia Jatar-Hausmann, *The Cuban Way: Capitalism, Communism and Confrontation* (West Hartford, CT: Kumarian Press, 1999), p. 77.

5. Although government exchange houses did not appear until 1995, the state was able to capture circulating dollars by selling imported goods at special dollar shops. See Jatar-Hausmann, *The Cuban Way,* for a good discussion of the dollar depenalization and its effects.

6. This cooperativization entailed a nominal decentralization of control to local administration, along with profit sharing among the farmers when profits existed.

7. Farmers' markets had been legal between 1980 and 1986. They were closed because they generated too much inequality and devolution of control for the regime's tastes.

8. Remittances have grown in recent years as the economic situation of Cuban Americans has improved and that of Cubans on the island has deteriorated. Foreign remittances are expected to reach nearly $1 billion annually at the end of the 1990s.

9. Economist Intelligence Unit (EIU), *Reassessing Cuba: Emerging Opportunities and Operating Challenges* (New York, 1997), p. 62.

10. CEPAL, *La Economía Cubana,* p. 253.

11. Cuba maintains an official exchange rate of one peso to one dollar. This rate is used for trade accounting and for certain transactions, such as when foreign companies exchange foreign currency for pesos to pay their Cuban workforce. The parallel market rate, the rate used at CADECA outlets, is set to approximate the market supply and demand for pesos and dollars. As such, it is intended to eliminate, or at least sharply reduce, interest in currency trading on the black market. By attracting the dollars from remittances and other sources into the state-run CADECA chain, the government is able to capture a greater share of the hard currency entering Cuba.

12. CEPAL, *Balance Preliminar,* p. 76.

13. A useful discussion of hard currency and related bonuses with extensive examples from the foreign enclave sector is provided in Philip Peters, "A Different Kind of Workplace: Foreign Investment in Cuba." Arlington, VA: Alexis de Toqueville Institution, March 1999.

14. Money owed to an enterprise but not yet paid is called an account receivable. Since the state owns most enterprises in Cuba, it can shift the accounts receivable among enterprises instead of providing support via a cash subsidy. This will lower the apparent budget deficit. The government can also arrange for the Central Bank to loan an enterprise money instead of making a subsidy out of the government budget. This, too, will lower the apparent budget deficit. At least until their switch to the Western system of national accounts (SNA) in the early 1990s, the Cubans kept a single con-

solidated government budget. If they did not begin keeping separate local and central government budgets when they adopted the SNA, this CEPAL observation would appear to be erroneous. If they did begin keeping separate budgets, the observation would appear to hold true.

15. CEPAL, *Balance Preliminar,* p. 75.

16. Rodríguez speech, op. cit. In 1998, the budget deficit equaled 550 million pesos, implying a GDP of some 22 billion pesos.

17. Speech of Osvaldo Martínez, op. cit.

18. There is an excellent discussion of the self-employed sector in Jatar-Hausmann, *The Cuban Way,* chs. 6 and 7.

19. See, for instance, EIU, p. 121.

20. EIU, p. 121.

21. Lage speech, op. cit. Translation by the author.

22. The EIU reports (p. 80) that labor costs in Cuba's FTZs vary from $1.10 to $6.00 an hour and that the minimum wage in the Dominican Republic is $0.61 an hour. The Cuban wage is calculated at the official exchange rate, which is the cost experienced by the foreign investor.

23. CEPAL, *La Economía Cubana,* p. 141.

3

After the Deluge?
Cuba's Potential
as a Market Economy

Manuel Pastor Jr.

What would Cuba look like after a transition? The question really involves two parts: the potential *path* of transition and the *end-state* of that process. In contemporary Cuba, the most likely avenues for fundamental change often seem blocked. Despite halting moves toward market liberalization, the government's commitment to reform remains less than halfhearted. While there was hope for a political opening in the wake of the Pope's 1998 visit to the island, the current political situation has become even less hospitable to alternative voices.

The end-state of any transition process is equally difficult to visualize. After all, the political and economic systems that replaced state socialism in Eastern Europe have exhibited several flaws, and the recent meltdown in Russia points to the risks inherent in any large systemic change. The Chinese model—a relatively far-reaching market opening accompanied by continuing restrictions on political freedom—may offer a better chance for economic success but has less appeal for those whose primary interest in Cuban affairs is the democratization of the island.

Yet systemic change will inevitably come to Cuba. The government's attempts to restructure the economy have yielded only modest results, but they have opened some space for new social forces that might be more interested in reform. The stresses and strains of the current approach, particularly the economic slowdown, will likely offer a new crack—one hopes in noncatastrophic conditions—for

policy and political innovations. Charting a course through these un-
certainties is a speculative but necessary task.

In this chapter I offer the following argument: First, Cuba has
followed a rather perverse form of stop-and-go reform in which success is immediately followed by backtracking. The reasons are political and such a policy cycle is likely to persist in the medium-term
future. Second, even in this context, it is possible to implement
measures that take into account the inevitable systemic transition
and thereby ease the costs when it comes. Third, even without such
measures, economic transition need not be as costly as it has been in
other locales. Certain factors, including the earlier dramatic fall in
Cuban GDP between 1989 and 1993 and the likely interest of outside investors, will ease the burden on output and employment.
Fourth, Cuba's comparative advantages are not clear-cut, suggesting
that, while a posttransition economy may not be mired in recession,
it will also not necessarily grow rapidly and well. Fifth, given the
long-term difficulties ahead, it is tempting to argue for a dramatic
change in the political system, its mid-level leadership, and its egalitarian values. However, incorporating elements of the existing leadership will help stabilize any future regime, and addressing distributional sensitivities would help to make any transition successful.

Slipping and Sliding
Economic Performance Since 1989

The Cuban economy was hit hard by the 1991 collapse of the Soviet
Union and the earlier erosion of the socialist trading system. Despite
attempts at economic diversification in the 1984–1989 period, exports of sugar and sugar products accounted for 77 percent of total
exports, and nearly 70 percent of the country's trade was with the
former Soviet Union. Domestic industry was dependent on inter-
mediate imports to fuel production (quite literally, in the case of oil)
and over one-third of foodstuffs were imported. Propping up this
fragile economic structure was Soviet largesse, specifically a willingness to offer favorable terms of trade and cover any trade deficits
with ruble-based loans. By the 1980s, this combination of price-
fixing and easy finance yielded the Cuban economy an effective subsidy worth over 20 percent of GDP.[1]

The changes in Eastern Europe wreaked havoc on this fragile and dependent structure, with various estimates placing the 1989–1993 fall in GDP at between 35 and 45 percent. To try to halt the erosion, the government adopted a somewhat contradictory combination of measures: first, a market-style promotion of foreign investment and tourism aimed mostly at relieving the foreign exchange crisis; and, second, heavy-handed rationing, labor mobilization, and economic planning to alleviate the consumption and production shortfalls in the domestic economy. The planners' portion of this strategy—including attempts to raise domestic food production and encourage biotechnology and pharmaceutical exports—is generally considered a failure. To give credit where it may be due, the Cuban government did manage to cushion the economy from the full extent of the economic shock, with GDP falling far less than the 70 percent shrinkage in import capacity. Unlike North Korea, for example, mass starvation in Cuba was largely averted, as the rationing system delivered a basic, albeit inadequate, diet, and the black market was eventually allowed to fill the rest of consumers' needs.[2] And while the government let its fiscal deficit soar to around one-third of GDP by 1993, it managed to keep certain priorities in place, with spending on education more or less retaining its share of the steadily shrinking GDP even as defense expenditures took a significant hit.

Still, by 1993, the government began to realize that deeper reform was in order. In August of that year, the government officially depenalized the use of dollars. While this was done partly to capture the remittance flows sent by U.S.-based relatives of island Cubans, it had the effect of sanctioning and facilitating existing black markets. In September of the same year, the government legalized limited self-employment and began a process of "cooperativizing" over 60 percent of state farmland, giving existing workers on selected state farms the right to lease their lands permanently. In October 1994, the government began to allow agricultural markets in which neither prices nor production was controlled. This was a significant ideological shift, since the previous incarnation of free agricultural markets had been closed in 1986 by Fidel Castro himself. In the same year, the government began cutting subsidies to state enterprises, raising the prices of state-supplied goods, and implementing new taxes.

These more systemic changes were correlated with the beginnings of a turnaround in GDP in 1994. While the accuracy of GDP measures in the 1989–1994 period is controversial, the official growth figures from 1995 forward seem reasonably on target and show a steady if unspectacular recovery during 1995 and 1996. In most countries in the developing and post-socialist worlds, this sort of positive result would have strengthened the hand of reformers and encouraged the government to stay the course with regard to economic strategy. There were indeed continuing signs of change, including the 1995 liberalization of foreign-investment regulations.[3] However, by 1996, the Cuban government began backpedaling from its own success, cracking down politically and economically. While other dynamics were present, including poor export prices and a new chill in U.S.-Cuban relations, the negative effects of this new policy on output growth can be seen in Figure 3.1.

Do I Have To? The Political Economy of Reform

What caused the slide in output growth and the slip in the pace of reform—and what implications do these have for any consideration of

Figure 3.1   Real GDP in Cuba, 1989–1998

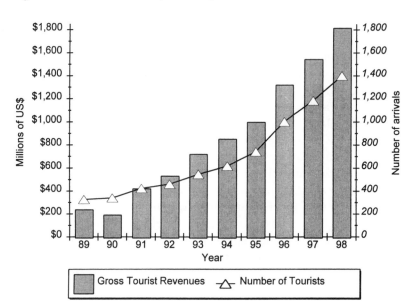

transition? As Dani Rodrik has argued, crisis can be an opportunity for major policy change.[4] For measures to stick, though, three things are necessary: The reforms must be designed and managed by capable technocrats; the reforms must scramble contemporary political alignments and thereby weaken organized resistance; and the "winners" from the reform process must materialize and mobilize as a political force quickly enough to support reformers through any loser-organized backlash. It is this sort of political-economy logic that has led some analysts to justify "shock" strategies for post-socialist transitions. Even if output costs could be moderated by a slower approach, delay gives political interest groups more time to organize and resist change, thereby derailing the economy from a long-range recovery path.

The island's economic reform has not followed this shock model. Cuban change has been gradual—even glacial—and the reason for caution has not come simply from the desire for a more economically sound approach. Rather, the government has been torn. It wants to see the economy recover, a goal that requires the acceptance to some degree of market logic. Yet the government has no real desire to see the reformers win, as it fears the creation of a new set of economic interests that would cause political difficulties further down the road. This fear has affected the coherence of the technical measures. The legalization of self-employment was followed by a series of restrictions and taxes so severe that the number of registered self-employed has fallen in recent years. The cooperativization of agriculture has occurred in the context of continuing requirements to sell a significant share of output to the state, and productivity growth in the new cooperatives has been unimpressive.[5] Tourism has been expanded but it has not been accompanied by the flowering of small businesses that might enhance the tourist experience. As a result, both spending per visit and the percentage of second returns are low by Caribbean standards.

The halfhearted commitment to change has been reflected in a stop-and-go cycle of reform. In most reform processes, economic success generally leads the reforming government to go further in its reform process. This presumes a desire for reform to succeed. In the Cuban case, macroeconomic recovery has tended to bring back-tracking: once the economy seems headed out of the woods, the government wants to run back into the socialist forest. This then leads to a slowdown in the recovery process, which winds up creating the material basis for yet another period of change.

Thus, while slowdowns like the one that occurred in 1998 will induce some policy change, they are not likely to produce a fundamental transition on the economic or political front. The government remains committed to socialism, with the introduction of market mechanisms seen as a necessary but temporary evil. There has been a rise in dissident activity on the island, but the government has shown little willingness to loosen the political reins. "Muddling through" seems the most likely course for the near future.

Getting There: Factors Affecting Transition

Despite the current impasse, a far-reaching transition will eventually come to Cuba as internal contradictions and external pressures mount. Some welcome the prospect of change, believing that a market system will reinvigorate economic energies suppressed by socialist regulations and therefore allow Cuba to realize its true potential for growth. At the same time, analysts recognize that transitions from state socialist systems have almost always entailed macro- and micro-economic costs, including declines in income, increases in inflation, and painful shifts in the distribution of income. What are the factors that would reduce or exacerbate the social and economic costs of change in Cuba?

The Macroeconomy:
Output, Inflation, Finance, and Investment

In a recent comparative analysis of liberalization and the behavior of output in former socialist states, Ernesto Hernández-Cata examines the transition process by developing and testing a model with two sorts of firms: a Type A firm making products that find markets under liberalization and a Type B firm making products deemed desirable under the previous socialist regime.[6] At least two factors lead to significant transition costs as the economy switches from one kind of firm to another. First, the mix of consumer demand in the transition is such that Type A firms face better relative prices and Type B firms face shrinking demand. Second, the efficiency in the

Type B sector is much lower, leading it to be more vulnerable to the foreign and domestic competition induced by market opening. The more dramatic the liberalization, the more significant the shock to the system and hence the higher the costs. Hernández-Cata also argues that the gains will be greater further down the road if liberalization is undertaken early and completely—although there is a bit less evidence that this is really the case for all liberalizers.

While any transition is likely to cause a reorientation of productive activity and perhaps a decline of investment and output in certain sectors, the aggregate costs of restructuring in Cuba could be lower than in other socialist transitions. State investment is already highly curtailed, and the dynamism of the economy (tourism, foreign investment, the small private sector) is coming from areas that might benefit by further reform. In one sense, Cuba has already experienced a large part of the usual transition recession via the dramatic fall in output that occurred between 1989 and 1993 (see Figure 3.1), and further decline may not be necessary.

In order to predict whether further decline would occur, I compared Cuba to a set of other developing, but capitalist, countries (see Table 3.1); inclusion in the sample was based on having a similar level of GNP per capita and all the data necessary for the comparison.[7] The Cuban figures are given for 1989 and 1993, the year for the reference sample and the year before the recent Cuban recovery began.[8] As with most socialist countries, Cuba in 1989 was over-industrialized in terms of both labor force allocation and sectoral share, and was therefore likely to see that sector shrink if liberalization took place. By 1993, however, the recession and lack of oil imports had downsized industry to a share similar to that of the reference sample. There was a significant shift toward service activities, suggesting that a new transition-induced industrial collapse would be less severe.

The trade share shrank considerably over the 1989–1993 period (due to the disruptions with the Soviet Union and the socialist bloc), but it is not terribly far off the sample and has been rising steadily in recent years. This suggests that trade "underopenness," which was a cause of recession due to trade shocks in other former socialist countries, may not be as strong a factor in Cuba's case; at the same time, the reduction in the trade share over the years examined indicates that Cuba may be less vulnerable to external shocks than it was at the beginning of its crisis. Recent events seem to have borne this

Table 3.1   Structural Indicators for Cuba Versus a Sample of Comparable Reference Countries

	GNP per Capita, U.S.$ from WDI	GDP per Capita, U.S.$ from HDR	Human Development Index
Sample, 1993	1,388	3,860	0.678
Cuba, 1993	1,450	3,000	0.727
	Labor in Agriculture	Labor in Industry	Labor in Services
Sample, 1993	35.9	22.5	41.5
Cuba, 1989	18.0	30.0	51.0
	Agriculture as % of GDP	Industry as % of GDP	Services as % of GDP
Sample, 1993	15.5	32.3	52.1
Cuba, 1989	14.2	45.5	40.3
Cuba, 1993	7.2	30.7	62.1
	Exports as % of GDP	Imports as % of GDP	Trade as % of GDP
Sample, 1993	18.3	30.2	48.5
Cuba, 1989	34.8	52.5	87.3
Cuba, 1993	14.2	23.4	37.6

Source: Data for reference sample from the UNDP's *Human Development Report (HDR)* and the World Bank's *World Development Indicators (WDI)*. The reference sample includes Algeria, Colombia, Dominican Republic, Ecuador, El Salvador, Guatemala, Jamaica, Jordan, Morocco, Papua New Guinea, Paraguay, Peru, and Tunisia.

out: the 1998 sugar harvest, the worst in over fifty years, slowed growth but did not force the economy into a full downturn. Overall, the pattern suggests that much of the pain has already been experienced and that further large recessions may not be necessary.

Of course, a transition-induced decline in GDP is still a distinct possibility. If Cuba opens and liberalizes, international competition is likely to force further industrial restructuring. Cuba really does have three distinct economies: a fairly massive Type B economy consisting of traditional public-sector firms; a small set of Type A firms that are oriented toward exports, tourism, and other internationally competitive sectors; and a growing informal economy that fills the gaps between the two.[9] The Type A firms are largely joint ventures in which foreign management expertise is critical. With some exceptions, most notably the investments by the Canadian firm

Sherritt in nickel and investments by other firms in telecommunications, there are too few opportunities afforded for the development of local entrepreneurs and managers, and hence little transfer of what might be termed management technology.[10] Moreover, the joint-venture firms currently have small impacts on employment, as they employ only 1–2 percent of the labor force.

Cuba would do well—that is, it would minimize the costs of future transition—if it were to expand the Type A sector, both by inviting in more foreign enterprise and by engaging in more space for self-employment and other Cuban private-sector initiatives. It is tempting to believe that such entrepreneurial energy and expertise already exists, with the currently self-employed ready and willing to take on the market when it finally arrives.[11] But learning how to *resolver* is different from learning how to produce; running a *paladar* (home-based family restaurant) is different from running a chain of restaurants; borrowing from extended family members to generate working capital is different from borrowing from a bank to purchase capital equipment. If local Cuban-owned businesses are to survive when the market arrives, it would be best to provide the incubator environment now, mostly by engaging in a staged privatization program (that is, starting with smaller enterprises while continuing to clean up the finances of larger state firms) and expanding the realm for self-employment.

Of course, a transition in Cuba would likely bring significant interest by Cuban American investors who, in turn, would bring business expertise as well as some familiarity with the culture. The downside of this is that a rapid influx of such investment could spur social resentment between island-based workers and Miami-based capitalists. One part of this tension could be racial, given the overwhelmingly European heritage of Cuban Americans and the more Afro-Cuban character of the Cuban population itself. In addition, sorting out the conflicting property claims of older Cuban American business owners could complicate and delay investment possibilities, an issue touched on below.

What about inflation? The Cuban economy is marked by excess liquidity—that is, extra cash held by residents simply because few domestically produced goods are available or desirable.[12] Given this swollen supply of money, price liberalization would quickly lead to a one-shot increase in prices (as excess cash chases scarce goods), but whether or not this becomes galloping inflation depends on whether the government exhibits macroeconomic discipline or laxity. The Cuban government has made significant progress in reducing its fiscal imbalance, and excess liquidity has been reduced slightly since its 1993 peak (and could be reduced further if the government used a mass privatization as a way to sop up excess pesos). Still, inflation remains a real risk, particularly because of the disjuncture between the official and market exchange value for the Cuban peso.

Cuba has tried to ease the pressure on the exchange rate. The government introduced a system of exchange houses in 1995, and the peso has been relatively stable for the past several years. Both the peso and the dollar circulate in the Cuban economy, with dollar shops having done $800 million in sales in 1998, and it is reported that Cuban firms and individuals have begun to hold some accounts that are convertible to dollars or other foreign currencies.[13] Still, full convertibility remains an objective, not an achievement of policy.

The financial structure in general can greatly affect the burdens of transition. Some reports put Cuba's external debt at just under $10 billion as of end-1998 while others suggest that it is nearly $11 billion. There has been a flurry of talks and negotiations in recent years, including restructuring agreements with Japanese and Italian commercial lenders, but the debt remains an obstacle (as does the U.S. embargo) to obtaining the medium-term finance needed to modernize domestic firms and equip them to make the transition from Type B strugglers to Type A survivors. Finance is also crucial for short-term trade prospects: one of the main variables restricting the contemporary growth of sugar and other exports has been the inability to obtain foreign credit for imported inputs. Transitional costs would be eased if Cuba could restructure its current debt and obtain new credit for firm restructuring.

The domestic financial system has seen some modernization and reform. A new Central Bank was established in 1997, and banking operations are on the way to full computerization. Cuban authorities report that Cuban banks, investment companies, and foreign lenders provided $1 billion in financing to companies operating on the island in 1997; such financial intermediation is increasingly important, as Cuban state firms are expected to reduce the level of government subsidies they require.[14] Still, the banking sector remains highly underdeveloped and mostly oriented toward the state, with the potentially dynamic microenterprise sector forced to rely on self-financing.

As for foreign investment, a variety of transnational firms have been involved in joint ventures, particularly in tourism, and investment flows do provide some foreign exchange relief. However, the level of committed and delivered foreign-investment flows has been relatively stagnant over the past few years. In more colloquial terms, "Cuba has hardly turned out to be the booming emerging market that some foreign companies had hoped when the island cautiously opened up to foreign investment several years ago."[15] Foreign investment would accelerate if a transition to a more market-oriented economy were occurring. If this was accompanied by a relaxation or elimination of U.S. restrictions on trade and capital movements, there would be a burst of interest by U.S. firms in general and Cuban American investors in particular.

However, such a happy result in terms of investment and growth is not a foregone conclusion. It is quite possible for Cuba to move closer to market rules without inducing a shift in U.S. policy. The latter depends on whether economic liberalization is matched by political change or whether Cuban reform occurs China-style, including sharp limits on political space and a seeming acceptance by entrepreneurs and the populace of the trade-off between economic and political freedom. Even if political conditions made it possible for the embargo to end and U.S. and Cuban American investors to enter, the initial rise in foreign investment might be dampened by squabbling in an underdeveloped legal system over prior and current property rights.

Public investment in infrastructure could help smooth the transition in several ways. On the one hand, it could make up for any shortfalls in aggregate spending by the government and private investors; on the other hand, it could pave the way for higher productivity by allowing for better roads, ports, railways, and so on. A large portion of such infrastructure development will need to be contracted out to foreign firms, in part to ensure that international standards are met (particularly with tourist-supporting infrastructure). The government will find it difficult to finance such spending, given its own need to trim budgets and the rudimentary nature of the tax system. Foreign aid will be important to support social safety nets (see below) and to develop infrastructure.

Finally, the conditions under which a transition takes place will greatly affect the economic consequences. If a transition to a more open economy occurs under some form of the current government, one could imagine conditions of relative political and labor peace, both of which would contribute to maintaining output and calming investor fears. If a political transition occurs involving some kind of cooperative shift of power to a new system, a degree of uncertainty might temporarily slow investment but the transition period would likely be short and investment would quickly recover. If the shift to a new system is violent, triggered by social protest over continuing austerity, discontent in the military, intra-elite struggles over Castro's successor, or other such events, there could be a significant lull in investor interest as things sort themselves out.

All this suggests that it would be best for the government to begin laying the groundwork now for transition by (1) expanding the realm of operation for Type A or private firms; (2) shedding labor in Type B or state (and cooperative) firms; (3) continuing to clean up fiscal imbalances; (4) developing an appropriate financial infrastructure; (5) making progress on price liberalization; (6) engaging in limited privatizations; and (7) deepening partnerships and linkages with foreign firms to ensure the transfer of technology and management expertise. Of course, this assumes that the government accepts the inevitability of a market-style economy and seeks to smooth the path in the interests of its citizens. As we have suggested above, the sorry truth is that reform is grudging. Privatization has been mostly ruled out and, while subsidies to state firms have been cut by 80 percent since 1993, modernization of this sector has been modest at best.

Microeconomic Costs: Employment and Distribution

Beneath the large macroeconomic aggregates lie the microeconomic shifts—for both markets and people—that will need to occur during any transition. The impact of transition on employment would be more severe than on output.[16] Part of the reason, noted above, is simply that the government has accomplished little with regard to rationalizing employment in state firms; thus, shedding labor would have little negative impact on production.[17] As a result, it will be possible to see economic growth with increasing unemployment, as happened in contemporary Argentina when it undertook its own (far more moderate) shift from state enterprises to the private sector.

The government could improve the situation by opening up more self-employment opportunities. The Chinese model of transition has dampened negative employment impacts by allowing the state (or

Type B) firms to continue operating with subsidies, mostly to serve as a source of labor absorption. The expansion of the private sector, first in agriculture, then in the rest of the economy, generated new employment but did not have the extra burden of needing to quickly absorb dismissed state workers. In this sense, China's state-owned industry has been a sort of social safety net that has generated a sense of worker security and allowed for more experimentation by individuals and the government. Cuba has had the security without the experimentation. The result is that transition could impose large employment losses even if output costs were minimal.

That worker security allowed for experimentation in China raises an interesting aspect of reform. A relatively equitable initial distribution of income can facilitate economic reform, partly because it leads to a sense (and reality) of shared burdens. While Cuba may have had some distributional advantages early in the adjustment process, these have largely been squandered over the past few years of halfhearted change.[18] Inequality has widened, with the reward system bearing little relationship to productivity and skills: bellhops and prostitutes earn more than doctors, those households with family members abroad do better than those without, and corruption pays since it brings access to dollar-earning and dollar-shopping.

This is the worst sort of inequality for maintaining reform. When those at the top of the earnings heap are more educated, skilled, and energetic, a certain degree of inequality may be seen as fair and general societal resentment is muted. When relative social status is decided by connections, chance, and the topsy-turvy rewards available in contemporary Cuba, it is bound to lead to resentment, rent-seeking, and short-term thinking and investment.

Transition will likely worsen the picture, and the longer transition is postponed, the worse the distribution of wealth will become. The relatively equitable income distribution characteristic of East Asian development was not really due to the frustration of market rules but rather to strategies—such as land reform, mass education, and incentives for firm-level job training—that led to a wider spread of physical, human, and financial capital. Placing the market on top of Cuba's current unequal distribution of assets will reinforce and exacerbate the current starting positions. Adding to the challenge will be Miami-based Cuban Americans and other investors who will be better able to take asset positions quickly owing to their relative wealth and investment expertise.

The government could help matters by spreading wealth in the form of a mass privatization of state assets to island Cubans in preparation for transition.[19] While the current government is unlikely to adopt such a course because it would decentralize economic power and signal a surrender to market forces, any transition government will need to consider how to preserve some modicum of equity in the distribution of assets, opportunities, and income even as it embarks on a path of privatization and economic opening. In general, an egalitarian commitment seems to be widespread among the Cuban people, and ensuring a proper social safety net will be crucial to transition.

Of course, Cuba has several broad advantages in any transition: First, its latecomer status means that it can learn from errors made in the previous transitions from socialist societies; second, the proximity to the U.S. market could help on the demand side; and, third, Cuban Americans comprise a ready group of investors eager to step into the breach of "decapitalization" wrought by the collapse of investment from over 20 percent of GDP in 1989–1991 to below 7 percent in 1994–1996.[20] Yet the advantage of the U.S. markets and Cuban American capital will not materialize if the Cuban government does not engage in political reform, the current sine qua non for ending the trade embargo and other restrictions. Major shifts in either U.S. policy toward Cuba or internal Cuban politics seem unlikely. As a result, an effective path to transition in Cuba remains obscure.

Being There: Cuba After Transition

Optimists suggest that Cuba's future is bright: Once a transition is launched, international trade and tourism will skyrocket, investor interest will rise dramatically, and high-quality Cuban labor will provide a solid base for long-term growth. The transition costs will soon be forgotten as Cuba launches an economic boom, one that will be significantly facilitated by a rapprochement with the United States and the (re)entrance of eager Cuban American investors.

In reality, the picture is more complicated. There are few solid statistics on Cuba's new economic structure, and it is difficult to determine where the island's competitive advantage may eventually emerge. One key strength stems from the "distortions" of Cuban socialism: its highly educated labor force and significant overspending (relative to other developing countries) on health and science. Biotechnology, for example, has achieved some degree of international competitiveness, with recent estimates suggesting that the sector may be contributing in the range of $125 to $150 million in foreign exchange earnings.

Yet biotechnology and pharmaceuticals face huge obstacles in that these industries are dominated internationally by a small number of large firms eager to suppress new entrants. Both sectors are also significant users of foreign exchange, suggesting that the macroeconomic gains will be limited. The best way to make progress in this area is to form alliances with large firms for development and marketing. Cuba has tried to do this, as evidenced by the SmithKline Beecham deal to test Cuba's meningitis B vaccine. Lifting the U.S. trade embargo would expand the market for Cuban pharmaceutical and medical products, with one Cuban estimate placing the potential market size at $500 million.[21] While this is a significant sum, it does not take into account the imports needed for pharmaceutical production or any market resistance that might be encountered from U.S. firms. Nor does the figure account for the fact that Cuba's competitive advantage in this area is based in part on researcher salaries that are extremely low by international standards; it is easy to imagine a brain drain resulting from the international integration that might accompany a transition.

Cuba will, of course, retain its usual comparative advantages in sugar, tobacco, and other products, all of which could be helped by the likely infusion of foreign technology and credit available in a posttransition economy. Sugar remains the island's most significant product, but it is one that lacks the expanding markets needed for healthy prices and profit margins (Figure 3.2). Lifting of the U.S. embargo might lead to enhanced sugar sales to the United States. However, access to the U.S. sugar market would probably be limited since U.S. import needs have fallen to 1.5 million tons from about 5 million tons in the early 1980s, and because Mexico now has special access to the U.S. sugar market via NAFTA.[22]

Tobacco represents a real opportunity, as Cuban products command the sort of profits available in niche markets. Nickel has been growing absolutely and as a share of total exports, and has the benefit of the Sherritt involvement.[23] Other products might bring strength— citrus, for example, could meet off-season demand in Europe (and

Figure 3.2   Composition of Exports, 1997

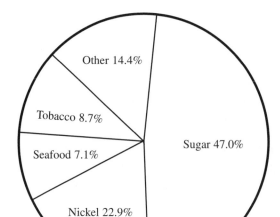

Other 14.4%

Tobacco 8.7%

Seafood 7.1%

Sugar 47.0%

Nickel 22.9%

possibly the United States if the embargo is lifted)—but the growth
in these sectors has been very slow. In any case, the dominant role
of sugar, hardly a market winner, will continue to constrain export
growth.

To explore this point further, consider the average growth in each
product category for 1995–1997, a period in which Cuba achieved a
relatively strong (by its earlier standards) 9.8 percent average annual
growth in total exports (Table 3.2). Suppose we wish Cuba to achieve
a 16.4 percent annual growth rate in exports over the next five years,
the level that Mexico's reformed economy was able to reach in the
1994–1998 period. Assuming that sugar revenues will grow no faster
than they did in 1995–1997—and this may be overly optimistic since
1998 production levels were actually the lowest in over fifty years
and 1999 prices slipped—nickel sales would need to rise by 35 percent a year (more than three times the current growth) or tobacco
sales by nearly 60 percent each year in order to achieve the target export growth rate.[24] Supply constraints are likely to prevent this:
nickel production may already have been largely rationalized (and is
a limited resource in any case) and tobacco is already experiencing
the sort of quality problems that could diminish Cuba's reputation

Table 3.2 Annual Growth Rate, 1995–1997 (percentage)

Exports	9.8
Sugar	8.9
Nickel	12.4
Seafood	2.1
Tobacco	22.4
Other	6.4

among cigar aficionados. No amount of economic liberalization is likely to significantly alter these constraints on production and growth.

Cuba has been working hard to expand its web of international trade ties. Cuba was a founding member of the Association of Caribbean States in 1994, and in November 1998 was awarded full membership in the Latin American Integration Association (ALADI). While ALADI is a mostly symbolic group in light of the rise of regional groupings like the North American Free Trade Agreement (NAFTA) and the Common Market of the South (Mercosur), the move was still important politically and reflects Cuba's growing trade with Latin American neighbors. Nonetheless, such intraregional trade is a minor part of Cuba's exports and will not yield much new demand. The real key would be an opening to the U.S. market, a result that would likely be dependent on political change in Cuba or policy change in the United States.[25]

Even with such an opening, growth in the external sector may be more likely to come from tourism, where gross revenues already exceed the sum of merchandise exports combined. As can be seen in Figure 3.3, the tourist sector has been growing rapidly. Cuba enjoys a beautiful coastline, a unique history, and a vibrant culture, all of which could stir tourist interest. Several studies predict that the lifting of the U.S. trade embargo could generate a significant rise in demand from new U.S. tourists.[26] However, a transition or posttransition government cannot simply assume that the opening of Cuba to the U.S. market would lead to a dramatic increase in tourist visits and spending. While visits by business investors and family members will probably grow, the current data suggest a very low rate of return visits. In addition, the curiosity factor that has led some to visit one of the world's last standing socialist regimes will disappear in a posttransition society, and a politically violent transition could

Figure 3.3 Tourism in Cuba, 1989–1998

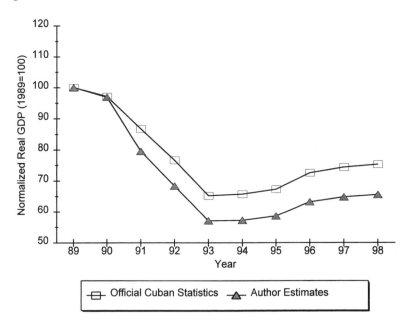

scare away visitors for years to come. Cuban authorities have acknowledged their frustration that spending per visitor is low by
Caribbean standards and actually seems to have been on a slight decline in the past four years.[27] Even under the best transition scenar-
ios, the government will have to make the investments necessary to
bring the tourist experience up to an internationally competitive
standard.

The second single largest source of foreign exchange in Cuba is
remittances. A transition is likely to see an increase in these flows as
regulations ease further on the U.S. side and Cuban émigrés become
eager to help their relatives through the difficult changes. Remittances are currently estimated to be between $600,000 and $800,000
a year, with reason to believe that the number is closer to the top end
of the band. The January 1999 easing of restrictions (U.S. citizens
are now allowed to send up to $1,200 a year to individuals and
groups in Cuba) could help increase the flow, although many Cuban
American families have been able to utilize other channels to send
funds to relatives.[28] Some believe that a jump in remittances could
also provide the finance needed for small businesses, at least in the

early years of transition. This would help alleviate any credit short-ages resulting from the underdeveloped financial system, particularly since even relatively sophisticated banking systems in the rest of Latin America have problems extending loans to small entrepreneurs.

Foreign-investment flows could also ease foreign exchange con-straints. However, investors will be nervous if the economy is not doing well in terms of the external sector. After all, foreigners want to repatriate profits in the form of their own currency, and unless overall external earnings are sufficient to ensure that this is possible, investment will lag. For this reason, the real performance of exports, tourism, and remittances remains crucial.

Aside from the external sector, what are the longer-term bases for growth? Whatever qualms might exist about the quality of Cuban data, health and education indicators are far superior to those for countries of similar GNP per capita. Most economic theories of growth point to the central importance of knowledge and learning, partly because this is key to the adaptation of new productive tech-niques. As a result, Cuba's high level of human capital should bode well for development. Some have suggested that, in the medium term, the high literacy rates and educational level of the average Cuban worker could stir investor interest in more sophisticated assembly-style operations, as in the *maquiladora* sector in Mexico where foreign inputs are imported and refashioned into exports using domestic labor and foreign capital.

Unfortunately, the free-trade zones Cuba established in 1996, partly in the hopes that foreign investors would use them to help modernize industry, seem to have attracted little more than ware-housing. While this is, to some degree, a function of insecure prop-erty rights under the Cuban legal system, assembly operations in a posttransition economy will not necessarily bring widespread growth, particularly since such factories in any country tend to shy away from local inputs and hence lack productive ties to the domes-tic economy. What is needed is closer integration with international productive structures—that is, having the Cuban portion of the as-sembly process be more integrated into a larger cooperative com-modity chain, as in the case of nickel.

In the longer term, there are serious problems with overestimat-ing how Cuba's high literacy and educational levels translate into labor productivity. Irving Louis Horowitz argues that "a creative and innovative people capable of repairing and modifying just about any artifact does exist. A people schooled in a computer environment with sound work habits does not exist."[29] While this may understate the capacity of Cubans to adapt to a new system, recent research applying growth models to Cuba does suggest that, despite the high level of education, the productivity of both capital and labor are extraordinarily low by international standards, particularly in agriculture.[30] Getting labor up to international speed will certainly be a transitional problem, but reforms and improvements in much of the educational and training structures are also necessary if Cuba is to achieve its long-term potential.

Policy Implications

Considering all the travails involved in moving to a market economy, would Cuba be better off to arrive there rapidly or slowly? Some have recommended that Cuba pursue massive and rapid systemic change. The argument in favor of such an approach is that it might immediately scramble the political calculus, diminishing the income and influence of certain groups and thereby weakening the political forces that have blocked reform. In this scenario, the price of liberalization is paid early and a more rapid return to growth is the happy payoff.

This sort of shock strategy for moving the country out of socialism will only come with deep political change. It is likely to involve a significant influx of Cuban American investors, a phenomenon that would introduce tension between island- and U.S.-based Cubans. It would also be likely to emerge in the context of a significant increase in U.S. influence over the island, which would also rub against nationalist sympathies. Finally, it is likely to involve few safety nets and significant distributional hardship.

An alternative approach is to slowly begin making the necessary alterations in the system's rules to limit costs and maintain political support for reform, recognizing that change is coming. Such an approach would represent an irrevocable commitment to a new economy while taking care to generate the institutional base necessary for reform. It would involve further development of the financial system, rationalization of state firms, expansion of self-employment, granting of ownership rights to cooperative farmers, development of antitrust legislation to prevent monopolies, extension of unemployment insurance, liberalization of prices, and so on.

In some ways, the gradual approach outlined above resembles the government's strategy of the past few years. There are two key differences: first, progress would be gradual not glacial, and, second, the government would be fundamentally committed to a market-oriented economy as the outcome of the reform process. This sort of approach could find some support among mid-level leaders in Cuba, many of whom are frustrated by current government policy, and could serve as the basis for a peaceful transition, albeit not one likely to make as much progress on the political front.

The gradual approach should also diminish the potential transition-related declines in output discussed above. Even if a shock approach is not taken, there will be production disruptions, and some sort of safety net, perhaps financed with external aid, would be necessary to avoid unrest during the transition period and allow the country to make it to the other side of reform. The Clinton administration promised as much as $6 billion over six years to facilitate a transition, but, as noted, this was largely dependent on political transformation accompanying economic reform. Such aid would amount to about 3–5 percent of Cuban GDP, depending on the exchange rate conversion. While the administration was right to note that this is a significant amount in per capita terms, it is useful to recall that the Soviet subsidy was over five times this level, suggesting that more might be needed to smooth the road to the market and ease political tensions. Of course, aid would be effectively supplemented by the easing of U.S. trade restrictions, a change that many observers feel should occur as soon as possible, with aid and other elements then made contingent on further economic and political change.

In any case, transition should be a goal of the Cuban government whether or not the United States reacts positively. In preparing for transition, Cuban authorities will have to acknowledge that state socialism has disappeared and that the best a socially minded leadership can hope for is a sympathetic and generous mixed economy. This embrace of the inevitable future would be signaled by the beginnings of privatization and the initiation of a dialogue with a Cuban American community that will certainly constitute an important element of the future investor class in the country.

For the United States, preparing for transition involves putting aside visions that the passage from socialism will be relatively painless and bring about a golden era of economic growth in Cuba. Markets may smooth resource allocation, enhancing efficiency and productivity, but the transition to a market economy is likely to be accompanied by serious disruptions and production shortfalls. Meanwhile, long-term growth will remain constrained by several factors, including the particular way in which the Cuban economy is inserted into the international economy (primarily via commodities and tourism), the fact that the island's much-celebrated stock of human capital will need significant adaptation to a market and internationalized system, and the need to upgrade the nation's physical infrastructure.

In the best of all policy worlds, both the United States and Cuba will see the light. The embargo will end and Cuba will make real and substantive reforms on both the economic and political fronts. Even under this optimistic scenario, the island will need substantial amounts of aid and investment—and the U.S. and Cuban American role in providing these resources will inevitably be controversial. A safety net will need to be created: transition must pay attention to distributional sensitivities or it will soon be derailed by political tensions. This will be a complex balancing act—one that will continue to challenge academic analysts and policymakers alike.

Notes

1. See the estimates in Manuel Pastor Jr. and Andrew Zimbalist, "Waiting for Change: Adjustment and Reform in Cuba," *World Development* 23, no. 5 (May 1995): 705–720. The calculation corrects for Soviet overpricing, as in Archibald R. M. Ritter, "The Cuban Economy in the 1990s: External Challenges and Policy Imperatives," *Journal of Interamerican Studies and World Affairs* 32 (fall 1990): 117–149.

2. Malnutrition was not completely avoided, as evidenced by the 1991–1993 outbreak of a neurological disorder that was largely attributable to inadequate diet. See Terence Monmaney, "Politics of an Epidemic," *Los Angeles Times,* November 20, 1995, p. A-1.

3. As Pérez-López notes, whereas the law really amounted to a codifying of various loopholes the Cuban government had allowed for years, the formal adoption was still quite significant politically. See Jorge F. Pérez-López, "Foreign Direct Investment in the Cuban Economy: A Critical Look," paper prepared for presentation at the First International Meeting of the Latin American and Caribbean Economic Association, Mexico City, October 17–19, 1996.

4. See Dani Rodrik, "The Political Economy of Policy Reform," *Journal of Economic Literature* 34 (March 1996).

5. Initial assessments were that the productivity of cooperatives was above that of state farms (see, for example, Carmen Diana Deere, "Reforming Cuban Agriculture: Toward the Year 2000," paper presented to the First Annual Meeting of the Latin American and Caribbean Economic Association, ITAM, Mexico City, October 17–19, 1996). The cooperatives' lack of productivity and market integration, however, seems evident. While the cooperatives held 58 percent of cultivated land in 1997, their share of sales in the free agricultural markets was 3.6 percent. Naturally, the private sector was overrepresented (73 percent of sales with 17 percent of land), but even state farms were doing better, capturing 24 percent of sales with 26 percent of land (see Carmelo Mesa-Lago, "The Cuban Economy in 1997–1998: Performance and Policies," *Cuba in Transition–Volume 8* (Washington, DC: Association for the Study of the Cuban Economy, 1998), p. 4. This suggests that quantity-style planning constraints were biting even harder on the cooperative sector than on the state farms.

6. Ernesto Hernández-Cata, "Liberalization and the Behavior of Output During the Transition from Plan to Market," *Cuba in Transition–Volume 7* (Washington, DC: Association for the Study of the Cuban Economy, 1997), pp. 198–215.

7. I specifically selected countries whose 1993 GNP per capita in dollars was between $1,000 and $2,000, and that had all the key variables. By most estimates, Cuba's dollar-value GNP per capita is somewhere in this range (see estimates in Nicolas Sánchez and Miles Cahill, "The Strengths and Weaknesses of Factor Analysis in Predicting Cuban GDP," *Cuba in Transition–Volume 8* (Washington, DC: Association for the Study of the Cuban Economy, 1998), pp. 273–288.

8. Not all data are comparable between the reference sample and the island economy. For details, see Manuel Pastor Jr., "Cuba: The Blocked Transition," *MOCT-MOST: Economic Policy in Transitional Economies,* vol. 8, 1998, pp. 109–129.

9. On the informal economy, see Jorge F. Pérez-López, *Cuba's Second Economy: From Behind the Scenes to Center Stage* (New Brunswick, N.J.: Transaction Publishers, 1995).

10. There have been management training programs introduced by the United Nations Development Programme and other official organizations, including Canada's Carleton University, but there is little substitute for the learning opportunities available in the joint-venture projects. See the discussion in Philip Peters, *Cubans in Transition: The People of Cuba's New Economy* (Arlington, Va.: Alexis de Tocqueville Institution, 1999), p. 6.

11. See, for example, the optimism in Philip Peters and Joseph L. Scarpaci, *Cuba's New Entrepreneurs: Five Years of Small-Scale Capitalism* (Arlington, Va.: Alexis de Tocqueville Institution, 1998).

12. According to Everleny Pérez, the monetary overhang fell from 11 billion pesos in 1993 to 9.3 billion pesos in 1995—and it has grown slightly but steadily since then, reaching 9.5 billion in 1998. See Omar Everleny Pérez, "Cuba: La Evolución Económica Reciente: Una Valoración," mimeo, 1998, p. 9.

13. In 1998, there were 1,123 outlets; effectively, the dollar shops have taken over the role of providing nonessential consumer goods to the Cuban

populace. Fifty-four percent of sales are now Cuban produce, up from 40 percent in 1997, and indicative of increasing integration of the country's productive structure into the dollar economy. See Economist Intelligence Unit, *Country Report, Cuba,* First Quarter, 1999, p. 19.

14. Subsidies to state enterprises are scheduled to end in 2002. Subsidies did fall in 1998, even though they were targeted for a slight increase. The government has eschewed privatization, but it decreed that enterprises must raise managerial standards to become self-financing and it set up a commission to develop plans for subsidy reduction in industry. By December 1998, ninety-five Cuban enterprises, including twenty that were export-oriented, were in this program.

15. See "Cuba: Business as Usual," *Business Latin America,* March 8, 1999.

16. The official unemployment rate is 7 percent, but some economists put underemployment at over 25 percent. The government earlier indicated its intention to dismiss 800,000 to 1 million workers from state firms, but union insistence that all displaced workers be provided training and new employment has slowed the downsizing.

17. Everleny Pérez, "Cuba: La Evolución," p. 17, indicates that state employment fell from 95 percent of total employment in 1989 to 77 percent in 1997. Filling the gap, according to Ritter, was the growth in the self-employed sector and nonstate agriculture, especially the state farms turned cooperatives (see Archibald R. M. Ritter, "Entrepreneurship, Microenterprise, and Public Policy in Cuba: Promotion, Containment, or Asphyxiation?" *Journal of Interamerican Studies and World Affairs* 40, 2 [1998]: 63–94). This cooperative sector, however, is inefficient and tightly controlled by state regulations; as a result, counting this as nonstate employment seems questionable.

18. Distributional data are hard to come by in Cuba. One indicator of the changing distribution of income is that, while 14 percent of account holders held 77 percent of the balances in December 1994, three years later 13 percent of account holders held 85 percent of the balances (Everleny Pérez, "Cuba: La Evolución," p. 10). The same author suggests that over 60 percent of the Cuban population is living in poverty, even controlling for sources of informal income.

19. See the plan offered in Pastor and Zimbalist, "Waiting for Change."

20. See Andrew Zimbalist, "Whither the Cuban Economy?" paper prepared for the Americas Society, May 10, 1999.

21. The estimate is from the head of the Havana Science Park, as reported in Economist Intelligence Unit, *Country Report, Cuba,* First Quarter, 1999, p. 20.

22. See "Cuban Access to U.S. Sugar Market Seen Unlikely," *Wall Street Journal,* February 16, 1999.

23. There was a 150 percent increase in the production of nickel and cobalt between 1994 and 1998; almost 50 percent of Cuban nickel production is coming from the joint venture, Moa Nickel, with Sherritt.

24. The calculations of required growth rates take into account compounding and the shifting composition of exports in a simulation model.

25. In January 1999, Cuban authorities estimated that the trade embargo cost $800 million, with costs coming in higher shipping costs, more expensive credit, higher import prices, lower exports, and currency losses.

26. See, for example, Nicolas Crespo, "Back to the Future: Cuban Tourism in the Year 2007," *Cuba in Transition–Volume 8* (Washington, DC: Association for the Study of the Cuban Economy, 1998). A study by Arthur Andersen (prepared for the Florida Trade Data Center) predicts that a lifting of the embargo would bring a doubling of tourist visits; see Ari Gaitanis, "Spain's Cuba Negocios Creates CN Bolsa Cuba Index," *Wall Street Journal,* May 13, 1999.

27. Part of the reason for the low spending is that about one-fifth of all tourists stay in rooms rented out in private homes. On the positive side, Cuba has been reducing the import content of the tourist industry.

28. See Jorge F. Pérez-López, "Economic Reforms in a Comparative Perspective," in Jorge F. Pérez-López and Matias F. Travieso-Díaz, eds., *Perspectives on Cuban Economic Reforms,* Tempe, AZ: Center for Latin American Studies, Arizona State University, Special Studies no. 30, 1998. See, also, "Analysts See Easing of U.S. Embargo on Cuba as Producing Little Impact," *Wall Street Journal,* January 7, 1999.

29. Quoted in "Struggling to Survive," *Dallas Morning News,* September 27, 1998, p. 11R. Perry, Woods, and Steagall are more optimistic that the Cuban "labor force will not require extensive retraining, especially in the export industries," but offer little evidence to back up this belief. See Joseph M. Perry, Louis A. Woods, and Jeffrey W. Steagall, "Alternative Policies to Deal with Labor Surpluses During the Cuban Transition" (Washington, DC: Association for the Study of the Cuban Economy, 1996), p. 93.

30. See Manuel E. Madrid-Aris, "Investment, Human Capital, and Technological Change: Evidence From Cuba and Its Implications for Growth Models," *Cuba in Transition–Volume 8* (Washington, DC: Association for the Study of the Cuban Economy, 1998), pp. 471, 477.

4

Castro's Cuba: Continuity Instead of Change

Jaime Suchlicki

As a new millennium begins, Fidel Castro faces mounting challenges to his regime on both the political and economic fronts. Popular discontent is growing, as evidenced by the number of Cubans seeking to leave the island and a series of defections by government officials and athletes. Pessimism, apathy, and cynicism have replaced revolutionary fervor, as Cubans have become increasingly disillusioned with the exhortations of the Communist Party and of Castro himself. Cuba's leaders seem to have lost the battle to create a new generation of Cubans devoted to the party and the revolution. After forty years of education and indoctrination, the "new man" is nowhere to be found.[1]

Economically, too, Cuba is under siege. The crisis triggered by the collapse of the Soviet Union—Cuba's main patron and the largest market for its goods—has been exacerbated by persistent structural problems within the economy, low prices for Cuban exports, and an inability to obtain sufficient foreign aid and imported oil. With low growth, scarcity of food, and popular apathy, the deepening crisis has led to a frenzy of planning and greater militarization in the hope of stimulating productivity and muddling through this difficult period.

Despite these political and economic difficulties, the Castro regime is likely to weather the current storm. The adoption of market-based reforms may well represent a solution to the economic crisis, but a full-blown reform process carries the risk that the government might lose control over society as well as the economy. In addition, profound reforms would also alienate some of the regime's key constituencies, such as party bureaucrats, sectors of the military, and those ideologically committed to Marxism-Leninism. These are risks that Cuba's leaders are not prepared to take.

As a result, the Cuban government has yet to demonstrate any significant resolve to embark on a path of market reforms. Instead, it has revived old strategies that have failed to generate real economic growth and has implemented new ones that are creating profound contradictions in society. Castro has called for Cubans to work harder, sacrifice more, and expect less in the years ahead. At the same time he is relying on tourism, remittances from abroad, and foreign investment to help his regime survive. While partially successful in bringing hard currency into the country, foreign remittances and tourism have accentuated the differences in society between those with dollars and those without, and have increased racial tensions, since most dollars are received by Cuba's white population.

When it comes to the prospects for reform, the contradictory statements and actions of Cuban officials can cloud the issue. There are some indications that Cuba is attempting to implement a slow transition from a command economy to a mixed economy composed of state-owned, private, and cooperative enterprises. Yet Castro and his hard-line supporters are resisting the adoption of any true economic changes, much less any political reforms.

Castro and the hard-liners recognize the need for economic recovery, but they also foresee the likely erosion of political power and control that would accompany the restructuring of the economy along free-market lines. While a vibrant private sector is essential for Cuba to achieve some measure of economic recovery, opposition to market reforms limits the extent to which the private sector can emerge and function effectively. For the foreseeable future, then, the economic crisis will continue and Cubans will experience greater austerity, more extensive food and consumer goods rationing, and much harder times.

Americans persist in believing that Cuba's economic crisis will lead to major political changes. The United States seems to be clinging to an outdated economic determinism in trying to understand and influence events in other societies and the calculations of their leaders. Neither punishment nor engagement has worked with Castro in the past, and neither is likely to work in the future. Despite growing economic difficulties and international pressure, Castro has not budged. Neither have the Cuban people rebelled to force out the present leadership. Disillusionment and alienation may be widespread, yet resistance or open defiance of the regime carries too high a price. Fearing repression and the possibility of long prison terms, Cubans seem resigned to await the end of the Castro era and the beginning of better times.

Predictions that the Castro revolution would follow the fate of other communist states after the collapse of the Soviet Union have been proven false, and the current regime is likely to remain in place even if the political and economic climate deteriorates further. Even after the island's leadership passes out of Fidel's hands, Cuba's transition will almost certainly be slow and painful. The strength and growing role of the military in the economy, a fairly monolithic Communist Party, and a vast and efficient security apparatus make it likely that the present political leadership and governing structures will continue to function and evolve slowly even after Castro's rule has ended.

The Economic Crisis: Origins and Response

Few anticipated the rapid and dramatic collapse of the Soviet Union and its empire in Eastern Europe in the early 1990s. Even fewer anticipated the end of communism in the Soviet Union. Western nations rejoiced at the spectacle of an independent and free Eastern Europe, the breakdown of the Soviet Union, and the development of a market-oriented and more open society in Russia.

For Cuba it was a devastating blow. Cuba lost not only the protective political umbrella offered by the Soviet Union, but also the economic support that had been its lifeline. Soviet aid and subsidies vanished suddenly. Access to Eastern European and Russian products at subsidized prices disappeared. The new republics demanded cash payments for their goods. The weakness and dependence of Cuba's economy became painfully evident.

The years that followed saw a deepening economic crisis in Cuba. Severe shortages of Russian and Eastern European petroleum, fertilizers, spare parts, raw materials, and foodstuffs crippled the economy. Without the availability of these subsidized products and without the money to buy them, the production of sugar, Cuba's main cash crop, declined to the lowest level since the 1959 revolution. Almost three-quarters of all factories on the island reduced or halted production for lack of spare parts and raw materials. Transportation and communications deteriorated rapidly, while foreign trade fell 70–75 percent. Unemployment and underemployment increased dramatically. The standard of living, already depressed, sank to new lows, bringing misery and suffering.[2] Hope for the future gave way to pessimism, despair, and a sense of alienation from the state. The Soviet-style economic model established on the island did not function without massive foreign aid, and there was no patron to replace the Soviet Union.

The government's initial response to the crisis in the early 1990s was to ration further the already limited supplies of consumer goods, to allow Cuban citizens to hold dollars and purchase goods in special stores previously reserved for tourists, and to increase efforts to attract foreign investment, especially in nontraditional industries such as tourism and mining. Deeper reforms, including cost accounting by enterprises, the establishment of investment funds by state firms, balanced budget and price liberalization, and the private ownership of property by Cubans, were contemplated but never implemented. Fearful of weakening his political control, Castro postponed these reforms indefinitely.

The government sought to survive by husbanding its meager resources. By 1993, rations had been reduced, labor brigades organized, security and repression increased, and heightened rhetoric used to boost morale and maintain social unity. Simultaneously, the military was given a greater role in managing and controlling the economy. Officers were entrusted with running agricultural and industrial enterprises and producing goods for themselves as well as for the population. Fidel Castro and his brother Raúl—head of the military, second secretary of the Communist Party, and designated heir—hoped that the militarization of the economy would bring order and discipline and reverse the deteriorating economic situation. At the same time, involvement in the economy provided a new mission to a military demoralized by the arrest and execution of several of its leaders and by the lack of purpose since its involvement in Angola in the 1980s.[3]

In response to deteriorating food production and concerns about growing social pressures, in 1994 the government permitted the establishment of farmers' markets at which agricultural products could be sold by growers directly to the public. Similar peasant markets had flourished for about four years during a difficult economic period in the mid-1980s as an experiment fostered by reformist elements within the regime. Castro, however, shut them down, claiming that Cubans were becoming "little capitalists" and that the egalitarian goals of the revolution were being undermined. The return to these "free agricultural markets" has helped alleviate critical food shortages by creating an incentive for individual farmers, working in cooperatives, to produce more and for state farmers to sell their surpluses in the open market.

Other economic reforms—apart from those related to foreign direct investment (FDI), discussed below—have been extremely limited and are designed to alleviate the most immediate problem facing the country, a lack of hard currency. Cuba has expanded the list of consumer goods that exiles can send to relatives on the island, and, in 1995, announced an increase in the number of visas that will be processed for travel from the United States to Cuba. The motivation for easing these restrictions is that Cuban Americans who travel to the island to visit their relatives usually bring with them money and nonperishable goods. If the Cuban government can encourage more exiles to visit the island or send money to their relatives, and if it can capture some of the dollars that now circulate in the black market, its hard-currency shortage will be eased.

These reforms have created sharp economic inequalities among Cubans. The new policies mainly benefit those who work in the dollar-earning sectors, such as tourism, or those who have generous relatives abroad. The policies have also heightened racial tensions, since most of those who receive dollars from their relatives abroad are white. In general, the black population has benefited much less from exile visits and dollar remittances, creating a latent hostility and resentment. The need for foreign exchange, however, is critical and, for now, Cuban officials are willing to accept the negative side effects of these policies.

These Band-Aid reforms, moreover, are not likely to lead to any noticeable improvement in Cuba's current economic situation and are readily reversible by the regime on short notice. In the Soviet Union and Eastern Europe, partial tinkering with state-run economies failed to provide sustained economic development. Only major structural changes and openings toward a market economy can hope to lead to this end. The Cuban leadership hopes that its partial reforms are sufficient to muddle through. If Cuba were again to receive large subsidies from a foreign benefactor or petroleum at subsidized prices, there would be no need for these reforms. The regime could then return to its preferred path of creating a Marxist society. But there is no benefactor on the horizon, and partial reform is likely to remain the order of the day.

The most significant response to the crisis thus far has been the reform of Cuba's foreign-investment laws and the country's active pursuit of joint ventures with foreign companies. It appears that Cuba would like to be as successful as China in attracting foreign investment, but it has yet to emulate the structural economic reforms that China has adopted, such as private ownership of land and the means of production. Cuban technocrats, as well as critics of the Castro government, have noted that there are significant differences between the two countries that work to the disadvantage of Cuba, such as size, natural resources, and labor productivity.[4]

Cuba is unlikely to be able to emulate the Chinese model of tight political control with regional market economies mainly because it will find it difficult to equal China's success in attracting foreign investment. China began its effort to attract foreign investors in the late 1970s and established a series of complementary economic reforms that supported this development strategy. Authorities created special regional economic zones in the early 1980s that combined material, fiscal, and labor incentives in strategic geographic locations. Not just firms, but individuals as well, were afforded greater freedom in economic decisionmaking. The Chinese focused their FDI efforts on manufacturing, with a particular emphasis on activities that would introduce new technology into the country. China permitted foreign firms to pay higher wages than those found in the rest of the country, rewarding and stimulating labor productivity increases. Workers resettled in these special areas and often remitted part of their earnings to family back home or sent them consumer goods purchased within those zones. The economic zones served as small islands of quasi capitalism within the larger socialist state. China was also able to attract significant investments into these zones from Hong Kong and Taiwan.

In contrast, Cuba has promoted investments in tourism as its highest priority and only recently began to promote investments in mining and manufacturing. Cuba has not yet attempted to link FDI with technology transfer. Nor has it permitted greater freedom for individuals in economic matters. While the Cuban government allows some workers to operate independently in small restaurants, repair activities, and other home-based enterprises, these activities are highly regulated. Unlike China, Cuba has not legalized large-scale private agriculture or manufacturing. Nor has it allowed foreign trade to take place independent of the state.

The Cuban constitution still outlaws foreign ownership of most properties and forbids any Cubans from participating in joint ventures with foreigners. Moreover, it is still illegal for foreign companies to hire Cuban workers directly. Foreign employers must pay the wages due to their employees directly to the Cuban government in hard currency. The Cuban government then pays the workers in Cuban pesos that are worth a fraction of the hard currency.[5] Furthermore, while the new foreign-investment law officially provides protection against government expropriation, all arbitration takes place within corrupt and arbitrary government institutions where little protection is given to the investor.

The Castro regime is unlikely to follow the Chinese model. Castro fears that any economic opening will lead to a political opening. He is concerned about Cuba's vulnerability due to the possible influence of the United States and its large Cuban American populations. He is also ideologically committed to a more restrictive political and economic line than the Chinese.

The Foreign Factor

After the collapse of the Soviet Union, Castro scrambled to create new international relationships, obtain foreign aid, and pressure the United States to lift its embargo, or at least to offer Cuba unilateral concessions. A number of Latin American countries have normalized diplomatic and trade relations with Cuba. Calls for Cuba's readmission into the Organization of American States are heard often, and democratic countries such as Colombia, Brazil, and Chile are willing to trade with and invest in Cuba. The English-speaking Caribbean countries, too, have welcomed representatives from Cuba to their meetings and an attempt is being made to integrate Cuba into the Caribbean Community (Caricom). Cuba was also invited into the newly formed Association of Caribbean States (ACS) over U.S. protests. Mexico has reaffirmed its long-standing relationship with the Castro government and, while relations are not as close as in the past, Mexico's current president, Ernesto Zedillo, has not reversed the direction of Mexican policy toward Cuba established by his predecessors. While criticizing Castro's human-rights record at the Iberoamerican Summit in Havana in late 1999, the Mexican president has also expressed his opposition to U.S. policy toward the island.

The immediate economic impact of improved foreign relations between Cuba and other Latin American nations is negligible. Only one-third of Cuba's meager foreign trade occurs with Latin America, and this is on a strictly commercial basis. Cuba, moreover, incurs a trade deficit with these countries, especially Mexico.

The political effects of improved relations with Latin American, as well as with European nations, may, however, be more important. Castro sees these countries' close relations with Cuba as a defeat for American policies and a way of isolating the United States. He hopes that Europe and Latin America will pressure the United States to offer unilateral concessions to Cuba regarding the lifting of the U.S. embargo and the possibility of U.S. tourists visiting the island. Yet during the past year, Europeans and Canadians joined at the UN to condemn Cuba's human-rights abuses and have been conditioning aid and investments to an improvement in human-rights conditions on the island. In early 2000, Castro withdrew from his attempt to join the Lomé Convention, complaining about European pressures.

The general trend among new democratic governments throughout Latin America as well as in Europe is to pressure the United States, albeit mildly, to change its policy toward Cuba. Some political leaders continue to believe that negotiations, economic inducements, and engagement will lead Castro to change his policies and allow for a peaceful political transition on the island. Optimistic appraisals of the possibility of a "deal" with Castro have been heightened by the spectacle of Cuba's ongoing economic crisis. This view holds that, as the crisis deepens, Castro will have no choice but to liberalize both the economy and the political system. Thus far, however, there is little evidence that either engagement or economic pressure will work. It can be argued that the onset of economic difficulties after the collapse of the Soviet Union led to some mild changes in Cuba to prevent a social explosion. Engagement by Latin

American and European nations and Canada, on the other hand, has led to little change. Efforts to engage the regime have come from other quarters as well: during a visit to the island in January 1998, the Pope criticized the U.S. embargo and called on Castro and the Cuban leadership to respect human rights and allow greater freedoms in Cuba. But the recent clampdown on dissidents and journalists suggests that the regime is ignoring the Pope's call for the Cuban leadership to open up to the world and serves as another indication of Castro's rejection of engagement.

One of the government's responses to the deepening economic crisis was tacitly to permit Cubans to flee the island. In 1994, thousands of Cubans attempted to leave in flimsy rafts and small boats. Many perished in the Florida Straits, while others reached U.S. shores. Most were captured by the U.S. Coast Guard and sent to the U.S. naval base at Guantanamo, located on the eastern end of the island of Cuba. After prolonged negotiations, most of the would-be refugees at Guantanamo were allowed to enter the United States in 1995. The deal called for Washington to provide 20,000 visas annually to Cubans seeking to migrate to the United States, while Havana promised to prevent illegal migration. The significance of this agreement was the reversal of the long-standing U.S. policy of allowing Cuban refugees to enter and remain in the United States. Rafters are now intercepted at sea and, unless they can show that they face persecution in Cuba, are returned to the island. While the massive exodus has stopped, the number of refugees arriving on U.S. shores continues to increase, creating a difficult situation in U.S.-Cuban relations, and the potential for a migration crisis directly into south Florida or into Guantanamo still looms on the horizon.

The Internal Factor

Since it assumed power four decades ago, the Castro government has shown no signs of making meaningful concessions in the political or human-rights arenas. Neither has there been any indication that Castro truly intends to open up the island's political system or promote a peaceful solution to Cuba's deepening crisis. History reveals examples of strong, even autocratic, leaders mellowing over time and softening their positions, but there is no evidence that this is the case with Castro. On the contrary, as the Cuban leader has aged he has become more intransigent and difficult. At the Fifth Party Congress in 1997, Castro reaffirmed his opposition to the United States and his unwillingness to relinquish power. Then, in February 1999, he introduced the most severe legislation that Cuba has ever experienced, sentencing dissidents, journalists, and others who deviate from the party line to between twenty and thirty years in prison.

While not representing an immediate threat to the regime, the numerous small groups that have proliferated in the past few years represent a potential threat if left unchecked. Nongovernmental organizations, religious groups, and independent journalists advocate a variety of reforms and freedoms that could undermine the regime and that Castro is not willing to tolerate. With the most recent crackdown, Castro served notice to his own supporters and to the population at large that he would not tolerate any dissent and that Cuba was entering a period of ideological orthodoxy guided by the Communist Party.

The 1999 legislation is an attempt to impose greater orthodoxy on the population and guarantee a smooth succession once Fidel has passed from the scene. On repeated occasions over the past several years, Castro has alluded to his mortality and to the need for the revolution to outlive him. Recent measures, including the crackdown on civil society and the replacement of key personnel, including Foreign Minister Roberto Robaina and Tourist Minister Osmani Cienfuegos, are part of a process to solidify power around his brother, Raúl, and to assure a smooth transition from himself to Raúl and then to others who will guarantee that the revolution continues.

Institutional Actors

Of the three institutional pillars of most communist regimes—the party, the military, and the security apparatus—in Cuba the party is the least important. The first reason is Castro's dislike of institutions. His style of leadership is personal, Stalinist, *caudillista,* and he views institutions as instruments for carrying out his policies rather than as policymaking bodies in themselves.

Second, the Communist Party (formerly the Popular Socialist Party, or PSP) played only a small role in the revolutionary struggle and was victimized by Castro in the early years of his regime. Castro, unlike European communist leaders, did not rise to power through party ranks, nor did he owe his successes to the party machinery. Even as the new Communist Party of Cuba was organized in 1965, it was a Castro creation, an attempt to legitimize an already existing communist regime.[6]

Third, since 1965 the relevance of the party has been limited. While major decisions in Cuba are discussed and made within the party's Politburo, it is Castro, and to a lesser extent his brother Raúl, who dominate this small body. Party congresses have been held at irregular intervals and then only to discuss and ratify preapproved policies.

Finally, the military, which preceded the party in its organization and development, is now not only independent from the party but superior to it as well. Neither personnel policy for the armed forces, nor military doctrine, nor internal control is handled by the party. Increasingly, military figures have taken key positions not only in the Politburo but also in other important party institutions. The militarization of the Communist Party is consistent with a trend toward the militarization of society at large.

The party continues to play its primary role as guardian of the ideological purity of the revolution and as a watchdog of other government institutions and the population at large. Key decisions are made within the party's 24-member Politburo, dominated by Fidel, Raúl, and their closest allies. Party commissions study important domestic and foreign issues of interest to the leadership and submit reports to the Politburo. Membership in the party carries status and respect, as well as fear, among the population. Entering this elite organization of approximately 600,000 members is a privilege reserved for the most loyal followers of the revolution.

The Fifth Party Congress

Those who expected major changes, or even minor initiatives, at the Fifth Party Congress held in 1997 were sadly disappointed.[7] The event was significant not for what took place, but for what failed to occur. Once more, as he has done for the past four decades, Castro showed that in Cuba politics dictate economic decisions. Despite mounting economic problems, the party did not introduce any major reforms that would propel Cuba into the market. Fearing that an economic opening might lead to political change, Castro rejected both. "We will do what is necessary," he said, "without renouncing our principles. We don't like capitalism and we will not abandon our Socialist system." Castro also reiterated his long-standing anti-American posture, accusing the United States of waging economic war against his government and calling for "military preparedness against imperialist hostility."[8]

Castro's long speech to the congress and the final party document reflected his determination to stay the course. Cuba's leader is intent on ensuring that his revolutionary legacy of anti-Americanism and Marxism-Leninism will outlive him. He showed determination and confidence that, despite the collapse of communism in Eastern Europe and Cuba's current difficulties, his hard line would be vindicated. Immediately following the party congress, Castro held a meeting in Havana of communist groups and leaders from all over the world to reassert the supremacy of communist ideology and to plan for a "comeback when capitalism fails." "Neoliberalism and globalization create consumer societies like the U.S. throughout the world," he emphasized, "and this is not a model for anyone."

The Fifth Party Congress was also important in that it reasserted Raúl Castro's position as undisputed heir to Fidel's dynasty. Both in private meetings and in public, Fidel praised his brother and summoned the faithful to support him so as to ensure the continuity of the revolution. While Raúl's official titles make him the obvious replacement for Fidel, it seemed that Fidel wanted to make clear to the party cadres and the larger population that his younger brother should be supported and obeyed, and that his leadership would be best for Cuba's future.

To reinforce his position as heir apparent, Raúl promoted an old-guard communist, Raúl Valdés Vivó, to become the new party ideologue in charge of education. Valdes Vivo is a former leader of the old pro-Soviet PSP, and Raúl Castro's political "godfather." It was Valdes Vivo who brought Raúl into the Juventud Socialista, the youth branch of the PSP, in the late 1940s, and introduced him to communist ideology.

In a speech closing the party congress, Raúl Castro also announced that the number of members of the central committee had been reduced from 225 to 150, and the Politburo from 26 to 24. The reduction would provide for a more efficient, streamlined party leadership. Several of the new members came from the armed forces, reflecting the growing trend toward the militarization of Cuban society.

The Military

The Cuban military is the most important institution in contemporary Cuba.[9] The military has achieved significant professionalism, legitimacy, and respect due to several factors. First, the Fuerzas Armadas Revolucionarias (FAR) are the heir to the rebel army that fought a guerrilla campaign against the Batista dictatorship in 1958. They emerged in 1959 as a nationalist force and only later became an internationalist army supportive of Soviet policies throughout the world. Yet, even then, and despite massive Soviet military aid, Castro attempted to maintain a semblance of independence from Moscow. In 1988 he established conditions for the Cuban military withdrawal from Angola and insisted that Cuban officers share with the Soviet and U.S. militaries the negotiating table that led to a peace accord in Africa.

Second, the Cuban population seems to have developed a degree of respect for the military. Cuba's armed forces are seen as the defenders of the nation and of Cuba's national sovereignty. They have refrained from involvement in internal repression and abuses, a job reserved for the security apparatus, thus escaping the stigma of the military under the Batista regime.

Finally, military sacrifices on foreign soil, particularly in Africa, are admired by large sectors of the population. This admiration, however, has begun to wane with the passage of time, as Cubans begin to question the direct benefits foreign involvement produced for their nation.

The military today, although smaller than during the Cold War, is a professional, technical, disciplined, and loyal force. Apart from the old guard, there is a new breed of well-trained and well-educated generals who were promoted in the 1980s and 1990s. Most of these officers are part of Raúl Castro's inner circle, having been nurtured and promoted by him. In exchange, they are fiercely loyal to their military boss. It seems clear to these officers that proximity to Raúl provides not only an avenue for upward mobility in the ranks but also protection from intrigue by other officers. The largest group of recently promoted officers is made up of generals and colonels who were too young to be members of the rebel army in the 1950s. Most of these men had no connections to prerevolutionary political parties or movements, and thus their affiliations and loyalties were formed after 1959. Coming from lower-middle-class or working-class backgrounds, and generally from provinces other than Havana, most of these officers are in their mid-fifties. There are increasing numbers of blacks and mulattos among the generals and colonels recently promoted. The average general has had at least three to four combat experiences on foreign soil together with numerous graduate and postgraduate courses in the best Soviet and Cuban military academies. Their field experience was gained in Vietnam, Angola, and the Middle East.

Within the ranks of the general staff, and moving from there to key civilian positions, are a group of highly professional technocrats associated with technological development, business, financial, and industrial administration, engineering, and logistics. The areas that since the 1990s have fallen under the jurisdiction of the military include tourism, telecommunications, technical industries, and sugar. Gaviota, Military Industries, State Reserves, Banca Metropolitana, Tecnotec, and others, in addition to civilian positions in the ministries of fisheries, sugar, merchant marine and ports, transport, telecommunications, and civil aeronautics, are in the hands of highly qualified technocrats emerging from the armed forces. Many of these technocrats come from the Air Force and Navy because of their expertise in the fields of complex technology, computer systems, international standards, and other specialized fields.

This military cadre has shown its willingness to follow Fidel and Raúl's views and commands. Either because of fear for their own safety, concern over a future without Castro, or shared ideology and power, they have generally remained loyal to Fidel and his brother.

The possibility of factionalism in the military is also diminished by the constant rotation of officers, which prevents the creation of personal loyalties within the services, and by tight supervision and control. This control is exercised through electronic surveillance and through the party and counterintelligence units within the military. Fear and distrust characterize the higher echelons of the military. It would be difficult for a disgruntled military leader to share his unhappiness with others or to plan any action against Fidel. Even if an unhappy officer were able to obtain the support of a few colleagues, it would be impossible for him to secure the support of a large number of military personnel whose loyalties and beliefs remain unknown. Successful rebellion within the armed forces is, therefore, unlikely.

Only in a situation of massive disturbances and popular upheaval in which the security apparatus is unable to establish order would the military be called upon to repress the population. If that were to happen, it is likely that factionalism, desertions, and unrest would occur within the military, hastening the collapse of the Castro regime. Until now, the Castro brothers have refrained from using the military and have used the security forces to deal with popular discontent, perhaps aware of the potential dangers involved.

The Security Apparatus

Unlike those of Eastern Europe, Cuba's security apparatus is monolithic and highly centralized. Castro learned well the lesson of Rumania, where forces from the Ministry of the Interior and the military fought each other. Castro has eliminated possible rivals within his military and security forces and placed the Ministry of the Interior under the control of the military, headed by an officer whom he and Raúl trust.

Among the Cuban people, there is strong belief in the efficacy of the security services and an overwhelming fear of their repressive capabilities. Castro has dealt harshly with real and potential enemies, executing them, sentencing them to long prison terms, or exiling them. He has infiltrated and destroyed opposition groups and prevented the development of any civilian group that threatens his authority. Recently, opponents of the regime have been given the choice of long imprisonment or exile.

Civil Society and the Opposition

Developing a civil society in a country jealously dominated by a political elite that has resisted change for four decades is not easy. Both Cuba's leader and the vigilant security apparatus see the development of a civil society as a major challenge to their absolute power on the island. Whether the limited gains made by a civil society independent of the Castro brothers in the past few years is the result of the collapse of the Cuban economy, the influence of outside forces, or a deliberate relaxation of control is difficult to know. It may be a combination of all three forces. Even with these gains, however, civil society in Cuba remains weak and ineffective, and is watched over carefully and constantly by the Castro regime.

In the past decade the Catholic Church has regained limited influence within Cuban society. The Pope's visit in early 1998 and his message *"no tengas miedo"* (do not fear) emboldened some Cubans and provided hope to others that the Castro regime would tolerate a broader opening for the church as well as for other groups. The honeymoon was short-lived. Although Castro declared Christmas an official holiday later that year, he failed to allow a significant increase in the number of priests on the island, refused the church access to the government-controlled media, and continued the prohibition on religious education.

Under these circumstances the church remains a weak adversary for the regime. The need to preserve its limited gains in a very difficult environment and to concentrate on religious rather than political matters weakens the role of the church as a major force for change now or during a transition. Although attendance has grown since the Pope's visit, the church has no access to the government-controlled media, no religious schools, and no national publication. Moreover, the number of priests, about 250 for a population of over 11 million, is extremely modest.

Other religious denominations have fared no better. Protestant groups have proliferated throughout the island, but they remain splintered and are devoted primarily to evangelical preaching. Afro-Cuban religious groups, the largest religious community in Cuba, command significant popular allegiance. Yet their structure of many small, independent groups and their strictly religious message limit their potential as a threat to the regime.

Apart from religious groups, the number of nongovernmental organizations (NGOs) has increased over the past few years. Most of these organizations were in fact created or encouraged by the Cuban Communist Party and are government-controlled or infiltrated by the security apparatus. These NGOs were created for two main reasons: first, to obtain assistance from legitimate NGOs in Western Europe, Canada, and even the United States, and second, to project an image that the Cuban regime was becoming more tolerant of dissent and allowing an opening to the outside world. Castro succeeded on both counts. Many in the United States and elsewhere have incorrectly seen the proliferation of NGOs as an indication that the regime is becoming less repressive, and they have provided increasing support to these groups.

Human-rights activists and organizations have recently received the brunt of government repression. In 1995, about one hundred small human-rights organizations came together under an umbrella organization called Concilio Cubano in an effort to present a united front against the Castro regime. Castro reacted violently, crushing the Concilio and arresting its major leaders. Since then many other prominent human-rights activists have been harassed, jailed, or sent into exile, and to date no other such organization has emerged. Independent labor groups have suffered similar fates. Aware of the impact of the Solidarity trade union movement in Poland and the potential strength of independent labor in Cuba, Castro has maintained tight control over the only government-sanctioned labor organization, the Confederación de Trabajadores de Cuba (CTC).

This is not to say that there is no opposition in Cuba. Opposition manifests itself in low productivity, disobedience of the law, alienation from the party and from the constant demands of the leadership, graft and corruption, and an increasing desire to leave the island. Independent groups of journalists and professionals, as well as religious organizations, have emerged under very difficult circumstances. Many of them have shown enormous courage in defying the regime. Small public demonstrations, clandestine publications, and distribution of foreign publications are partial manifestations of opposition to the system. Yet, time and again, the security apparatus has infiltrated these groups and eventually discredited or destroyed them.

Fearing the system's repression and the possibility of long prison terms, Cubans seem resigned to await the end of the Castro era and the beginning of better times. Disillusionment and alienation may be widespread, but open defiance carries too high a price.

After Castro: Continuity or Change?

The possibility of regime continuity seems stronger for Cuba than it has been for other communist states. Although their end came

suddenly and swiftly, it took decades of decay to weaken critically
the regimes of Eastern Europe, and Soviet disengagement and acceptance were required to hasten their collapse. In Poland, where
Solidarity was born in 1980 as the first nongovernmental trade union
in communist history, a military-led government took control and remained in power for a decade. In China, the communist regime obtained a new lease on life following Mao's death in 1976, initially
through Deng's reforms and then ultimately through increased repression, particularly against student protesters.

In Latin America, many noncommunist authoritarian regimes
held out for decades in the face of external pressure and internal
weakness—among them, Trujillo's regime in the Dominican Republic, Somoza's dynasty in Nicaragua, Pinochet's dictatorship in Chile,
and the Institutional Revolutionary Party (PRI) in Mexico. The latter case is particularly instructive. Despite profound financial and
economic crises and the erosion of popular support for the official
party, the PRI-based regimes have remained sufficiently strong to
stay in power, even as they have radically altered Mexico's economic course.

The Castro regime is bound to draw lessons from the mistakes
made by other communist regimes, such as the toleration of Solidarity in Poland, the gradual openings in Czechoslovakia and Hun-
gary, the rivalries between the military and security forces in Rumania, and the electoral defeat of the Sandinistas in Nicaragua. It is
also likely to incorporate the lessons offered by the Chinese experience, such as maintaining military control over key sectors of the
economy and pursuing only gradual economic opening. While these
models may be instructive, it is doubtful that Castro needs any foreign example to influence his predilections for how to govern or to
reinforce his dislike for democracy and the electoral process.[10]

For Cuba, the problem of succession is crucial. No totalitarian
regime has been able to devise a smooth system of transition, and
Castro's disappearance could touch off an internal power struggle.
Most likely, however, such a struggle would take place within the
revolutionary ranks rather than outside them. Despite Castro's overwhelming presence, it seems doubtful that the revolution will collapse when he dies or becomes incapacitated. The stability of the
regime is based primarily on the strength of the armed forces, undoubtedly the most vital of the three pillars on which the revolution
stands. The other two, the party and the security apparatus, serve

under increased military supervision to control, mobilize, socialize, and indoctrinate the population. The organization and strength of the civilian bureaucracy that has grown up around these institutions seem to assure the continuity of the revolution. Thus, while Castro is unquestionably the motor that drives the revolutionary momentum, with a replacement the machinery might slow down but still continue to work. Some Cubans may accept Castroism without Castro because of the threat of force; others because they fear losing the gains in housing, health, and education they have received in the past; still others because of anti-Americanism or commitment to a Marxist or nationalist ideology

A revolt against Castro's rule in the absence of large-scale outside intervention seems highly unlikely, especially as long as the Cuban armed forces remain loyal to him and to their immediate commander-in-chief, Castro's brother Raúl. The continued loyalty of the armed forces appears highly likely. Not only are they a Castro creation, but they also have developed a large measure of professionalism, are thoroughly integrated into the political system, and enjoy an important and trusted role in the nation's general economic management. While Fidel's harsh criticism and punishment of some of his officers stationed in Grenada, the prolonged Cuban presence in Africa, and the execution of General Ochoa caused some stress within the military, these events did not lead to increased instability within the Cuban government.

During the process of institutionalization that culminated in 1976, Raúl was officially appointed second to his brother in every position within the party and the state: second secretary of the Central Committee of the Communist Party of Cuba, first vice president of the Council of State, first vice prime minister, and vice president to the National Defense Commission. During the Fifth Party Congress, held in 1997, Fidel reiterated publicly that Raúl would be his successor. Several weeks later he backed off, stating that it was not within his rights to appoint a successor and emphasizing that in Cuba there were long-standing institutions fully empowered to make that choice. Although he is adhering to the legality of the process, it is clear that Castro wants power to pass to his brother, and nobody in Cuba is likely to challenge that decision.

Upon Fidel's death, the Politburo would propose to the Council of State a new successor as first party secretary and president of Cuba. The council would debate the recommendation, vote, and pass it on to the National Assembly of Popular Power (NAPP), calling an extraordinary session for this purpose. The assembly then would debate the proposed candidate and vote, ratifying the candidate to make him president. This process could take several days, during which, of course, the "second-in-command" would be in charge. It is likely that once the presidential candidate and party secretary, probably Raúl, is proposed by the Politburo, all other persons and institutions would support the decision.

Another possible scenario is that upon Castro's death or incapacitation, and as part of a proposal emerging from the Politburo, a redistribution of power could be implemented. A new first party secretary, most likely Raúl Castro, could be appointed. This is a party decision and does not require any confirmation or ratification by the Council of State or the NAPP. The Politburo could also make a proposal for presidential succession. Raúl could be appointed to this position or, more likely, Ricardo Alarcón, president of the Popular Assembly and a longtime ally of Fidel and Raúl, would become president. In 1998, Alarcón declared that if asked he would be ready to assume the presidency, a statement he would not have made without the approval of the Castro brothers.

Under this scenario, real power would remain in Raúl's hands. He would not only be first party secretary, but also continue as commander in chief of the armed forces. Alarcón would carry on the more ceremonial duties of the presidency, a task that Raúl seems to dislike. This shared power arrangement could help the regime survive any succession crisis since it would preserve the existing institutional strength of the regime. While some analysts argue that a government structured like this would collapse, probably because of internal divisions or popular discontent, it seems likely that this new model—based on efficient control rather than charisma, enjoying the support of the military and the party, and probably providing for mild economic changes—could continue for an indefinite period.

There is no guarantee, however, that the younger brother will survive the older one. If both Fidel and Raúl are gone from the scene, different factions within the party and the military would attempt to fill the void. A collective leadership made up of members of both groups seems the most likely outcome, with the military playing a dominant role.

Aware of his advancing age, Fidel has become increasingly preoccupied with the succession question. In numerous speeches, he has alluded to his mortality and, particularly during his long speech at the Fifth Party Congress, emphasized his concern with a smooth transition to his brother's leadership and his desire that the revolutionary foundation he has built survive his disappearance and even that of Raúl.

Anti-Americanism, nationalism, internationalism, and totalitarian control remain the basis of this foundation. For more than a half century, since the days he distributed anti-U.S. propaganda in Bogotá in 1948, Castro has opposed the United States. For forty years, he has kept complete control of Cuba and has supported a variety of revolutionaries, terrorists, *guerrilleros,* and mercenaries throughout the world, most of them avowed enemies of the United States.[11]

Internationalism is one of the policies that Castro cherishes. He continues to travel extensively in Africa, Latin America, and Europe, seeking support for his revolution and criticizing U.S. policies worldwide. Violent support for anti-American groups, however, has diminished since the shutting down of the Soviet protective umbrella. This is not to say that old connections and commitments have completely disappeared. Castro remains close to guerrilla groups in Colombia, the Palestinian Liberation Organization in the Middle East, the Spanish Euzkadi ta Askatasuna (ETA), and the Movement for the Liberation of Angola, ready to support them within his limited resources and capabilities.

The electoral victory of Castro's old friend Hugo Chávez in Venezuela offers Cuba an important ally. Chávez will pressure the United States to change its policies toward Cuba, will support the island's reintegration into the Latin American system, and will oppose any Latin American condemnation of Castro's human-rights violations. But more critical to Cuba is the possibility that Chávez could provide Castro with long-term credits or subsidized prices to purchase Venezuelan oil. This would help bail out the Cuban economy, enabling Castro to continue to muddle through a difficult period.

Uppermost in Castro's mind is the preservation of his legacy. He contemplates with horror the possibility that, once he disappears, Cuba might return to the U.S. orbit, or the Cuban revolution could collapse amid civil war and chaos.

It is in this context that we must understand Castro's recent actions, especially the crackdown on dissidents on the island. The Castro revolution is entering a critical stage. Not unlike Mao before his death, Castro is unleashing a cultural revolution in Cuba. Although clearly not as violent as the Chinese cultural revolution, the goal is the same: to ensure, strengthen, and preserve Castro's legacy.

Castro has been encouraged in this course of action by several events in addition to Chávez's victory in Venezuela. First, the spectacle of Russia's economic difficulties and possible chaos has increased hopes within the Cuban leadership for a return to communism in that country or for a friendlier leadership. The rise to power of Vladimir Putin in Russia has the Cubans hoping for increased trade and economic relations. Second, the Chinese, despite their economic reforms, have maintained a steadfast totalitarian political course and shown a willingness to close ranks with Cuba and other communist regimes. Third, the growing strength of the Fuerzas Armadas Revolucionarias de Colombia (FARC) in Colombia could provide Cuba with a key strategic and economic ally if a power-sharing agreement is reached between the FARC and Colombia's president, Andres Pastrana.

Internally, Castro sees little challenge to his regime. Despite mounting economic difficulties, Cubans have not rebelled. The disorganized and sporadic demonstrations that have taken place on the island in recent years have been easily repressed by Castro's security apparatus. The dissident movement, while growing, poses no major threat to the system. The impact of the U.S. people-to-people policy on the dissident movement has been small, and for that matter Canada or Europe's policy of engagement has had very little effect. While the economy has not improved significantly, the bottom may have been reached, and Cubans have adjusted to the new economic realities.

With his recent repressive actions, Castro has once again shown that in Cuba political considerations are paramount. He risked upsetting the mild thaw in the Clinton administration's U.S. policy toward Cuba, trade deals with the European Union, and condemnation by the world community over increasing human-rights abuses in order to achieve his objectives: maintaining complete political control and ensuring a smooth succession of power and the long-term survival of his revolution. There is every reason to expect he will continue to seek the same objectives in the years ahead.

Notes

1. Introduced by Castro in the 1960s, this concept called for a change

in the values and attitudes of most Cubans. Allegiance would be transferred from the family to the party and the fatherland. The influence of the church would be eliminated. Devotion to the cause of communism would prevail. Man would consciously labor for the welfare of society, and the collective interest would supersede the individual one. The young would be taught to respect party leaders and to obey party discipline. The new man would develop the characteristics of Castro's Rebel Army in its fight against Batista, including abnegation, a spirit of sacrifice, courage, and discipline.

2. See Jorge Pérez-López, "Cuba's Socialist Economy: The Mid-1990s," pp. 225–256; and Carmelo Mesa-Lago, "Cuba's Economic Policies and Strategies for the 1990s," pp. 177–203, in I. L. Horowitz and J. Suchlicki, eds., *Cuban Communism,* 9th edition (New Brunswick, N.J.: Transaction Publishers, 1998).

3. The 1989 arrest and execution of General Arnaldo Ochoa, together with other officers, on trumped-up charges of drug trafficking and corruption created significant discontent within the military. See José Alonso, "The Ochoa Affair and Its Aftermath," in I. L. Horowitz and J. Suchlicki, *Cuban Communism,* pp. 626–663.

4. See Jaime Suchlicki and Antonio Jorge, eds., *Investing in Cuba: Problems and Prospects* (New Brunswick, N.J.: Transaction Publishers, 1994).

5. For example, if the government charges $100 per worker, the worker will be paid 100 Cuban pesos, since the government maintains an equal official exchange rate between the U. S. dollar and the peso. In reality, however, the U.S. dollar is exchanged on Cuba's black market at the rate of 25 pesos to $1. The worker, therefore, receives $4 per month, while the government keeps the other $96.

6. See Michael Radu, "Cuba's Transition: Institutional Lessons from Eastern Europe," *Journal of Interamerican Studies and World Affairs* 37, no. 2 (summer 1995): 83–111.

7. See Jaime Suchlicki, "The Party Goes On," *Cuba Brief* (Freedom House, winter 1997).

8. *Granma,* October 9, 1997.

9. For a comprehensive analysis of various aspects of the military, see Jaime Suchlicki and James Morris, eds., *The Cuban Military Under Castro* (Coral Gables: Institute for Cuban Studies, 1989).

10. See Edward González, *Cuba: Clearing Perilous Waters?* (Santa Monica: Rand Corporation, 1996).

11. For penetrating studies of Castro's personality and objectives see Georgie Ann Geyer, *Guerrilla Prince: The Untold Story of Fidel Castro* (Kansas City: Andrews McMeel, 1993), and Tad Szulc, *Fidel: A Critical Portrait* (New York: William Morrow & Co., 1986).

5

Why the Cuban Embargo Makes Sense in a Post–Cold War World

Susan Kaufman Purcell

As the Cold War recedes further into history, critics of the U.S. embargo against Cuba have stepped up their campaign to have it lifted. First, they argue, it is a relic of the past that has proved unsuccessful, since Fidel Castro remains in power. Second, they claim that it is making it difficult for Cuba to undergo a peaceful transition from Castroism to a democratic political system. Instead of the embargo, they are pressing for a new policy of engagement with the Castro regime.

These attacks on the embargo are based on several erroneous assumptions. By classifying the embargo as an anachronistic holdover from the Cold War, its critics imply that the embargo has remained essentially unchanged since Washington first imposed it in 1961. This is both misleading and untrue. Since the end of the Cold War, both the focus and nature of the embargo have changed. In contrast to its initial goal in 1961 of containing Soviet and Cuban communism, today its goal is to help level the playing field between the Castro government and the Cuban people in order to facilitate a transition to democracy and a market economy.

The embargo's critics also assume that the policy they wish to substitute for the embargo is new with respect to Cuba. In fact, the opposite is the case. Engagement is precisely the course that Canada, Western Europe, and Latin America have taken toward the Castro regime. It has been no more successful than the U.S. embargo in removing Castro from power or in moving Cuba toward democracy and a market economy.

Unfortunately, few people realize that today's embargo is not the same as the original Cold War embargo. Nor do they focus on the fact that engagement with Cuba has been tried by other countries and has failed. This is because the debate over the embargo has usually been a debate over U.S. policy toward Cuba, not over the policy of other nations toward the island. Since the United States has played the role of odd man out by refusing to normalize relations with Cuba, the embargo's critics have only had to show that U.S. policy toward Cuba has not worked. They have not had to establish that the engagement policy of other countries has been successful.

The time has come to correct these misunderstandings. It is no longer useful to compare the Cold War embargo of the United States with a hypothetical post–Cold War U.S. policy of engagement. Instead, the debate must be refocused on the present U.S. embargo as compared to the current policies of engagement pursued by other countries toward the Castro government.

Such a comparison will show that today's embargo is a considerably more fine-tuned policy than was its Cold War predecessor. It allows and encourages increased contacts and communication between the Cuban and American people. It also targets the flow of resources to private citizens and nongovernmental groups on the island instead of to the Castro regime, thereby leveling the playing field between the Cuban people and their government. This represents a considerable loosening of the embargo on a people-to-people level. Simultaneously, however, the embargo has been tightened in order to make it difficult for the Castro regime to replace the billions of dollars in lost Soviet subsidies received during the Cold War with foreign loans, investments, and trade. By doing so, Washington hopes to facilitate a transition to democracy on the island by making the Cuban people less dependent on the Castro government and better able to challenge the political status quo.

In contrast, the policy of engagement that the embargo's critics support is as untargeted as was the original U.S. embargo of Cuba. It would not discriminate between the Cuban government and the Cuban people. Instead, it would allow the overwhelming majority of the new resources entering Cuba from the United States to go to the Cuban government, rather than to the Cuban people. The result would be a further strengthening of the Castro regime and an indefinite postponement of Cuba's transition to democracy.

The Post–Cold War Embargo

The U.S. embargo against Cuba,[1] imposed two years after the Cuban revolution, was originally expected to cause the collapse of the communist regime of Fidel Castro. By the mid-1960s, however, after the Cuban leader obtained Soviet military and economic support, it became apparent that the embargo would be considerably less effective than originally anticipated. As a result, Washington shifted gears and redefined the embargo into a tool for containing Fidel Castro and his efforts to spread communism throughout Latin America and other third world countries.[2]

The Soviet collapse in 1989 ushered in the post–Cold War era. It also marked the beginning of the end of Moscow's generous subsidies to Havana, which are estimated to have averaged between $4 billion and $6 billion annually. Many observers concluded that the Castro regime would be unable to survive the demise of the Soviet Union. Their assumption proved incorrect, in part because trade with Western Europe, Canada, and Mexico began to replace lost Soviet aid. Conspicuous among those companies trading with the Castro regime were subsidiaries of U.S. multinational corporations located in these areas. The value of such trade was estimated at $700 million per year.

Congressional opponents of the Castro regime were eager to discourage other countries, as well as U.S. subsidiaries, from trading with Cuba. Congressman Robert Torricelli, a Democrat from New Jersey, therefore introduced, and Congress subsequently passed, the Cuban Democracy Act of 1992. The law prohibited subsidiaries of U.S. corporations from trading with Castro's Cuba. It also prohibited foreign vessels that had entered Cuban ports for purposes of trade from loading or unloading freight in the United States for 180 days. In an effort to deprive the Cuban government of dollars, the act tightened restrictions on the kinds of U.S. citizens who could spend money in Cuba without permission from the U.S. Treasury. It also sought to discourage, and thereby reduce, the flow of dollars to Cuba by requiring individuals seeking to send money to relatives on the island to get licenses from the U.S. Treasury's Office of Foreign Assets Controls.

The tightening of the embargo represented the "stick" side of the Torricelli bill. There was also a "carrot" side that authorized the U.S. president to waive the prohibitions on foreign subsidiary trade or the restrictions on third-country vessels trading with Cuba if and when he determined that the Castro government had held free, fair, and internationally supervised elections. In addition, the Cuban government had to have given opposition parties time to organize and campaign, allowed full access to the media, shown respect for civil liberties and human rights, and moved toward a market economy.

The third set of provisions of the Cuban Democracy Act, known as Track II of the Torricelli bill, involved efforts to strengthen civil society so as to facilitate a democratic transition in Cuba. Track II allowed expanded telephone and mail service to the island, as well as visits to Cuba by academics, journalists, and other specialists.

Opponents of the U.S. embargo in Congress and in academia in particular criticized the Cuban Democracy Act as "more of the same." They regarded the bill, which was strongly supported by pro-embargo forces in the United States, as a continuation of a Cold War policy in a post–Cold War age. In reality, however, the bill reflected an effort both to grapple with the Castro government in the aftermath of the Soviet collapse and to align U.S. policy toward Cuba with Washington's post–Cold War policy toward Latin America. The latter now emphasized support for democracy, human rights, and market economies. During the Cold War, in contrast, U.S. policy had often favored anticommunist military regimes over democratically elected left-wing governments.

The Cuban Democracy Act was the first building block of the post–Cold War embargo. It tightened U.S. sanctions against the Castro government while taking some small steps toward engagement with the Cuban people. The hard-line provisions of the bill were premised on the belief that, in the absence of the Soviet subsidy, Castro's days were numbered. The Cuban Democracy Act was aimed at accelerating his removal from power. In the meantime, however, the embargo continued the policy of containment in order to keep Castro from threatening U.S. interests in Latin America and elsewhere. The embargo's critics argued that containment no longer made sense, since Castro had ceased supporting guerrilla forces in Latin America. What they failed to realize, however, was that the Cuban government had not had a change of heart, but rather a change of economic capability. Without the Soviet subsidy, the Cuban government did not have enough money to aid forces in Latin America and elsewhere that were hostile toward the United States, such as guerrilla groups operating in Colombia and Peru. With resources,

Castro could still do significant damage, given the fact that Latin America's new democracies were extremely fragile and that the region's democratic transition was occurring during an economic crisis that obliged these governments to radically restructure their economies, bringing considerable hardship to the population.

The Cuban Democracy Act took effect in 1992, the same year in which Soviet aid remaining in the pipeline dried up. The hard-line provisions of the act accomplished some of their goals. The Cuban government admitted that, by July 1993, the law had raised the island's shipping costs by 42 percent. The Institute for European–Latin American Relations (IRELA) found that, by December 1993, the act had cost Cuba approximately $1 billion as a result of the higher prices that Cuba had to pay for imports and because of increased difficulties in exporting.[3]

During 1993, the first year in which the Torricelli bill was in force, the Cuban government initiated a series of economic reforms aimed at attracting foreign capital to the island. Between 1993 and 1996, the Cuban government allowed Cubans to hold and use dollars and other hard currencies. It also permitted self-employment by individual Cubans in more than one hundred job categories and approved the creation of free farmers' markets and a number of retail markets for handicrafts and surplus products made by government enterprises. The government also encouraged foreign investment, especially in the tourism industry. In its desire for capital without capitalism, however, the government prohibited foreign companies from directly hiring and paying their Cuban workers in hard currency. Instead, the companies agreed to relinquish the hard currency for workers' salaries to the government. Through its use of an artificial exchange rate, the government then kept almost all the hard currency for itself while turning over a small amount to the workers in pesos.

Cuba's welcoming of foreign investment, in addition to some of the other reforms such as the legalization of the use of dollars, suggest that the Torricelli bill has had an impact on the regime. Although Cuba's need for hard currency was undoubtedly a more direct cause of the Cuban government's limited economic opening, the Cuban Democracy Act nevertheless obliged Cuba to make more extensive economic reforms than it had originally intended, as it exacerbated Cuba's hard-currency shortage by increasing its costs of production and trade.

Evidence that the tightening of the embargo in 1992 hurt Cuba also comes from the Castro regime's very energetic campaign, following the passage of the Torricelli bill, to have the embargo lifted. During the Cold War, Castro and his colleagues had repeatedly minimized the embargo's impact, claiming that they did not care whether it remained in place or not since it was ineffectual. Immediately after the Soviet collapse, the Castro government did not seem too preoccupied by the embargo, as trade between Cuba and U.S. subsidiaries partially offset the loss of Soviet trade and aid. Following the implementation of the Cuban Democracy Act, however, which prohibited such trade, Cuban officials announced that the removal of the embargo was their number-one international priority.[4]

Although the tightened embargo hurt the Castro regime, the government found ways to offset some of the damage. The limited economic reforms that the Cuban government implemented following the Soviet collapse succeeded in increasing Cuba's access to a portion of the hard currency required to keep the economy functioning, although at a low level. The reforms made it attractive for foreign companies to invest in sectors such as mining, tourism, and telecommunications without encountering competition from U.S. firms. In addition, Cuba's economic difficulties and its inability to enter the U.S. market allowed these foreign companies to drive a hard bargain with the Cuban government. As a result, foreign investment on the island increased dramatically between 1993 and 1996.

Cuban American congressmen were particularly disturbed by the fact that many of these foreign investments involved former U.S. properties that the Castro government had confiscated shortly after it took power. By agreeing to invest in properties that had been "stolen" from their U.S. owners, these foreign investors were seen as profiting from Castro's illegal behavior at the expense of the former U.S. owners. The combination of the inflow of foreign capital (which helped offset Cuba's loss of Soviet aid) and its use of expropriated U.S. property led Congress to pass the Cuban Liberty and Democratic Solidarity (Libertad) Act, or the so-called Helms-Burton bill, in February 1996. President Clinton had initially opposed several of its provisions on the grounds that they either would not stand up in court or would alienate U.S. allies abroad. He ultimately signed the legislation, however, following the shoot-down on February 24, 1996, by Cuban aircraft in international waters of two small private planes piloted by Cuban Americans.

The bill, which was strongly supported by Congress, passed in the House with a 336 to 86 vote and by a margin of 74 to 24 in the Senate. It was signed by President Clinton on March 12, 1996. Its two most controversial provisions are also the ones that have had the most impact in discouraging foreign investment on the island. Title III enables U.S. nationals to bring lawsuits in federal court against foreign governments, companies, and individuals who "traffic" in expropriated U.S. property. It also gives the president the power to delay implementation indefinitely, six months at a time, if he believes that a delay would be in the U.S. national interest and would facilitate a democratic transition in Cuba. Title IV denies entry into the United States of foreigners who traffic in expropriated property claimed by U.S. citizens. Those potentially affected include corporate executives, owners, controlling shareholders, and their immediate families and agents. Exceptions can be made for medical reasons or to contest legal action taken against them because of their trafficking.

Another important provision of the bill initially received little attention although it significantly curtailed the president's autonomy regarding Cuba policy. Helms-Burton codifies—or transforms into law—all existing economic sanctions against Cuba, including the 1961 embargo and the 1992 Cuban Democracy Act. Prior to Helms-Burton, most of the sanctions, including the embargo, were the result of executive, not congressional, decisions. Until the passage of the law, a U.S. president could have lifted the embargo unilaterally. It will now require an act of Congress to change the embargo.

The Cuban Liberty and Democratic Solidarity Act, as its formal name indicates, closed loopholes in the embargo and encouraged a democratic transition on the island. Taking its lead from the earlier Cuban Democracy Act, it authorizes several million dollars of aid to be provided by the United States once Cuba holds free, fair, and internationally supervised elections that do not result in either Fidel Castro or his brother Raúl remaining in power. The latter condition, while technically undemocratic, reflects the strong antipathy toward and distrust of the Castro brothers on the part of several key U.S. legislators.

The sanctions against third parties trafficking in confiscated U.S. properties have been strongly attacked, particularly by the European Union, Canada, and Mexico, whose nationals have invested relatively heavily in Cuba. Although the earlier Torricelli bill had also had an extraterritorial reach, in that it prevented U.S. subsidiaries based abroad from investing in Cuba, the foreign outcry in that case was hardly noticeable. This is probably because the Torricelli bill's extraterritorial reach allowed foreigners investing in Cuba to do so in the absence of U.S. competition. The bill therefore rewarded foreign companies while hurting American ones. The extraterritorial provisions of Helms-Burton reversed this situation, which may explain why it has been so heavily criticized abroad. It helped U.S. citizens whose properties had been confiscated by the Castro government, while penalizing foreign companies attempting to invest in these properties. The law does not, however, slap sanctions against all foreigners investing in or trading with Cuba, as some critics imply. If no U.S. claims against the property exist, the provisions of Helms-Burton are irrelevant and the investment can proceed without fear of U.S. sanctions.

Despite, or perhaps because of, the controversy surrounding the third-party sanctions provisions of Title III of Helms-Burton, President Clinton has delayed their implementation for consecutive six-month periods since the bill became law in 1996. This has led some critics to conclude that the sanctions now lack credibility and, as a result, have lost their ability to deter foreigners from investing in Cuba. This is doubtful. As long as a U.S. president retains the power to implement Title III sanctions, foreign investment in these assets will remain a risky economic venture. Adding to the uncertainty, there is some doubt whether Title III could survive a court challenge. Specifically, some legal experts argue that the provision allowing Cuban Americans to bring lawsuits in U.S federal court against foreign governments, companies, and individuals who traffic in properties they owned when they were Cuban citizens is of dubious legality. In view of these considerations, postponing implementation of Title III makes sense. It keeps the threat of sanctions intact, while avoiding a court battle that the U.S. government might ultimately lose.

It is still too soon to reach definitive conclusions regarding the impact of Helms-Burton, although a provisional assessment is possible. On the one hand, the costs of the policy to the United States have been significant. It has created ill will between the United States and its friends. It has also put Washington, rather than Havana, on the defensive for its policies. On the other hand, Helms-Burton seems to have made it much harder for Cuba to attract foreign investment since 1996. The Castro government no longer provides detailed information regarding foreign investment in Cuba on the grounds that doing so would put investors at risk because of Helms-Burton. Foreign newspapers and magazines, however, do occasionally report investments in the energy and tourism sector.[5] The reports, however, are few and far between, and are offset by sporadic announcements of companies that decided against proceeding with planned investments.[6]

Foreign companies' decisions against investing in Cuba are known only because they originally announced their intention to invest and subsequently changed their minds. The number of companies that never announced their plans to invest in Cuba but were planning to do so and subsequently shelved such plans because of Helms-Burton is impossible to determine.

Furthermore, the law has clearly aggravated Cuba's liquidity crisis by discouraging foreigners from lending money to the Cuban government out of fear that the money might be used for projects involving confiscated U.S. properties. As a result, the Castro government has been obliged to borrow capital at higher interest rates and for shorter periods, principally from Western European lenders. Finally, since the implementation of Helms-Burton, Cuba's economic growth has declined dramatically. It fell from 7.8 percent in 1996 to 2.5 percent in 1997. In 1998 economic growth did not exceed 1 percent. A rate of 6.2 percent is estimated for 1999. The increase is mainly due to an improved sugar harvest, a performance that may not be sustainable in 2000 because of a delayed start to the 1999/2000 harvest due to weather problems.

Clearly, the U.S. economic embargo is only one of the factors that accounts for the relatively low level of foreign investment and economic growth in Cuba. More significant are the government's own economic policies, especially its continuing commitment to "Cuban socialism." Another contributing factor is the absence of checks and balances to protect investors against arbitrary and sudden decisions by the government. Nevertheless, the inability of Cuba to trade with, and receive investment from, the United States because of the embargo exacerbates the negative impact of Cuba's economic and political policies and institutions.[7]

Critics of Helms-Burton and the embargo in general assert that Cuba's economic decline diminishes prospects for a democratic transition on the island, while increasing the probability of the outbreak of violence. The reality, however, has been somewhat different. Since the end of the Cold War and the disappearance of Soviet subsidies, Cuba's economic difficulties have obliged the government to implement precisely the kinds of economic reforms that Castro himself recognizes could weaken his grip on power and lead to a democratic transition. On the other hand, once the government managed to obtain enough foreign capital to enable it to avoid an economic collapse, it postponed additional reforms indefinitely. At the same time, it also severely circumscribed or reversed those reforms that had made individual Cubans less dependent on the state. For example, when the government feared an economic collapse in the early 1990s, it allowed small independent private businesses to be established, despite the threat that Castro feared they might present to his continued control. Once the economy showed signs of recovery, however, the government severely increased both its taxation and regulation of these businesses. As a result, many of these businesses failed, thereby reducing the potential threat that independent entrepreneurs could pose to the government.

The most recent changes in the embargo have focused on the engagement side of the policy—specifically, the strengthening of civil society in Cuba in the context of a tightened U.S. embargo as a result of Helms-Burton. In March 1998, two months after Pope John Paul II's visit to Cuba, the Clinton administration streamlined visa and licensing procedures for travel between Cuba and the United States by qualified individuals, such as academics, other than senior Cuban government officials. The two exhibition baseball games held in Havana and Baltimore in 1999 between the Cuban national team and the Baltimore Orioles were a direct result of this measure. Whereas before the administration only authorized flights between Miami and Havana, the United States now allows flights from U.S. cities other than Miami to destinations in Cuba other than Havana. All U.S. residents, not just those with relatives in Cuba, may send up to $1,200 annually to individual Cuban family households, and larger amounts may be sent to Cuban organizations that are independent of the government. Washington also authorized the sale of food and agricultural inputs to private entities and farms in Cuba and proposed the restoration of direct mail service between the United States and Cuba, as well as the establishment of postal money order service.

Many critics of the embargo have ridiculed the supposed hypocrisy of those who support the tightening of the embargo while simultaneously "undermining" it by sending money to relatives and friends on the island. The critics are missing the point. There is nothing hypocritical about wanting to deprive the Castro government of resources, while strongly supporting the transfer of resources to individual Cuban citizens and nongovernmental groups and organizations. This is, in fact, the essence of the post–Cold War embargo. It no longer penalizes both the Cuban government and the Cuban people, as it did during the Cold War. Instead, it seeks to contain the Cuban government by depriving it of resources, while simultaneously increasing contact with the Cuban people through the transfer of resources.[8]

Why Lifting the Embargo
Would Help Castro and Hurt the United States

The fact that the U.S. embargo against Cuba has changed since the Soviet collapse has not had much impact on the policy's opponents. They continue to assert that the embargo has failed and that it is time to "try something new," by which they imply full engagement with the Castro government, as well as with the Cuban people. They bolster their argument by pointing out that the embargo has been in place for almost four decades and Fidel Castro is still in power. Although they cannot guarantee that the lifting of the embargo will prove any more successful in bringing about a democratic transition from Castroism, they argue that it makes sense to replace a failed policy with one that has brought success elsewhere and has not been tried in Cuba.

There are several problems with the argument of the embargo's opponents. One is that it is debatable whether a policy of engagement has worked elsewhere. Engagement has been tried most spectacularly with the communist regime in China. While it has helped to modernize China, it remains unclear whether it will produce a peaceful democratic transition. What is obvious is the regime's continued determination and ability to crack down on groups considered threatening to the political status quo. Vietnam is another example of a communist regime whose political system remains undemocratic despite some liberalization in the economic sphere.

There is, of course, the case of communist Eastern Europe. According to opponents of the Cuban embargo, years of engagement with the West were decisive in overturning communism there. While contact with the people of Eastern Europe undoubtedly helped them in their fight against their governments, after the Soviet collapse many of them were quick to point out that the West's engagement with their communist rulers had prolonged, rather than accelerated, communism's decline by providing the regimes with resources and a degree of political legitimacy. Instead, they argue, the inability of the Soviet Union to suppress its own popular uprisings is the real explanation for the transition to democracy in the former Eastern Europe.

Finally, there is the case of the Soviet Union. Did it implode because of engagement with the West, or because it felt threatened by the Strategic Defense Initiative of the Reagan administration and proceeded to pour its limited resources into strengthening its defenses, bankrupting the country in the process? Again, there is no single cause for a regime's collapse; some explanations, however, are better than others. In fact, it is impossible to resolve the argument, since there is no way to reproduce the Soviet collapse in a laboratory under controlled conditions. As a result, ideology remains the best predictor of an individual's position regarding the Soviet collapse. More liberal observers will place greater emphasis on the beneficial impact of engagement, while more conservative ones will stress the impact of an aggressive, hard-line policy toward Moscow.

Comparing the Castro regime to existing communist regimes, or to those that collapsed fairly recently, however, is misleading. Cuba is still governed by the man who led the Cuban revolution, while these other communist regimes had or have moved to a more institutionalized form of communist rule prior to their transitions. For this reason, it would be more accurate to compare Castro's Cuba with China under Mao, Vietnam under Ho Chi Minh, Eastern Europe under its original communist rulers, and the Soviet Union under Stalin. Using this criterion, only Rumania was characterized by both communism and personalistic rule at the time of its collapse. Engagement with the West, particularly with the United States, probably prolonged Ceauşescu's regime and led to the only violent transition from communism to democracy in Eastern Europe.

It is not necessary, however, to focus on countries such as China, Vietnam, the former Soviet Union, and communist Eastern Europe in order to decide whether or not engagement with communist governments is an effective policy. We can look at Cuba itself. The United States is the only major Western country that has not followed a policy of full engagement toward the Castro regime. Europe, Canada, and Mexico in particular have prided themselves on pursuing a more enlightened and effective policy for encouraging a democratic transition on the island and repeatedly have urged Washington to follow their lead.

What have these countries achieved as a result of their policy of engagement with the Castro regime? Very little, except for the gratitude of their private sectors for enabling them to invest in Cuba without having to worry about competition from their U.S. competitors. In some cases their private companies have earned substantial profits. During the first several years of investing on the island, the head of the Sherritt Corporation of Canada, which has made substantial investments in Cuba's mining and tourism industries, missed no opportunity to taunt the United States for its misguided embargo policy, which allowed Sherritt to reap large profits from its investments. More recently, he announced that, as a result of meager returns combined with bureaucratic red tape, Sherritt will divert approximately $35 million of intended investment from Cuba to other countries.

On the political side, the governments of Western Europe and Canada in particular made a number of efforts, both public and private, to persuade the Castro government to improve its human-rights record and to implement democratic reforms. Their entreaties were roundly criticized and rejected by the Cuban leader, who categorized their efforts as infringements of Cuba's sovereignty.

It is puzzling why European and Canadian leaders believed that Castro would change his behavior or the nature of his regime in response to their requests that he do so. There were not, after all, any conditions attached to the engagement policy. Instead, the European and Canadian governments indicated exactly the opposite—that is, that their willingness to engage Cuba was not conditioned on the behavior of the Castro government. The Cuban leader may be an autocrat, but he is not stupid. If foreign countries are willing to allow their citizens to invest in Cuba under rules that greatly benefit the Cuban government at the expense of the Cuban workers, who receive only a portion of the money that these companies pay the government to cover wages, that is fine with him.

One explanation as to why advocates of full engagement believed their policy would be effective relies on the common assumptions regarding the magic of the markets. Since many supporters of engagement are economic determinists, they believe that engagement ultimately leads, although perhaps slowly, to decentralization, first of economic resources and then of political power. This assumption is problematic because it makes politics the dependent variable. In other words, the argument assumes that governments cannot shape the economic environment in which they function but, instead, merely reflect the economic forces operating in a particular country. In some political systems, however, especially highly undemocratic ones, politics is more often than not the independent variable, while economics is the dependent variable. The degree to which politics is the independent variable depends on the degree of political and economic centralization that exists in a particular regime.

Fidel Castro's Cuba is a prime example of a highly centralized system. Politically, there are no important independent groups, with the possible exception of the Catholic Church. But the church's continued independence hinges on its avoidance of politics. If it were to become more overtly political, the regime would almost certainly quickly curtail its freedom of action. With regard to the rest of society, there are no independent labor unions, private-sector organizations, or political parties. There are also no independent newspapers and there is no freedom of the press. The government owns and controls all the key industries in the country and all the natural resources. The government even decides how much of which crops must be sold to the government by private farmers.

It stands to reason, therefore, that a regime so concerned with controlling its own citizens would be equally concerned with controlling the behavior of foreign investors. When Castro needed foreign capital in the aftermath of the Soviet collapse and the termination of Moscow's aid, he encouraged foreigners to provide capital in a way that would offer the least threat to his continued control. Specifically, he forced foreign companies to allow the government to choose their workers and to keep almost all the hard currency that these companies paid the government to cover their workers' wages. The foreigners accepted his conditions, probably in the belief that their presence would unleash new forces in society that would eventually change the nature of the regime into something more democratic. In fact, acts of defiance against the regime began to increase and the internal opposition began to organize and grow. The foreigners were correct in the first part of their assumption: Cuba began to change as a result of the influx of foreign capital and the increased foreign presence. The foreigners were incorrect, however, in believing that there was nothing that Castro could do to stop such change. When the Castro government unleashed a wave of repression in 1996 and again in 1999 against human-rights and prodemocracy leaders, the foreigners compounded their error by verbally condemning the political crackdown but doing nothing to reassess the efficacy of their policy engagement.

The Canadian government is the only exception. In April 1998, Canadian Prime Minister Jean Chrétien made an unprecedented visit to Havana in the hope of encouraging Castro to open up Cuba's political system in return for Canada's criticism of the U.S. embargo and pursuit of a policy of engagement with Cuba. The prime minister was publicly criticized and humiliated by the Cuban leader, who rejected his appeal to release four leading dissidents from jail and used the visit to lambast the United States while the prime minister stood at his side. The incident triggered calls in Canada for a reevaluation of Ottawa's policy toward Cuba. It is possible that Canada will conclude that a policy of unconditional engagement is doomed to failure and, instead, will condition further aid and investment along the lines of the so-called Sullivan Principles, which held foreign companies investing in South Africa to a higher standard of behavior than that practiced by the South African government. Specifically, the Canadian government could insist that Canadian investors be allowed to hire and pay their Cuban workers directly in hard currency. If the Canadians were to be joined by other countries whose citizens invest in Cuba, it might prove effective. Such a change would help free Cuban workers from their dependence on the state, thereby strengthening civil society on the island.

Unconditional engagement makes sense only if there is something other than an undemocratic government with which to engage. In the absence of private groups, unconditional engagement will not level the playing field. Instead, it will tilt the status quo in the direction of the already too-powerful government and further reduce the possibilities for a democratic transition.

Can the Embargo Be Sustained?

During the Cold War, few people in the United States challenged the wisdom of the embargo. Since the Soviet collapse, however, pressure to reexamine the policy has been growing. One reason is the gap between expectations and reality. Supporters of the embargo had not expected the Castro regime to survive the termination of Soviet aid. The fact that Castro is still in power, despite the cutoff of aid and the tightening of the U.S. embargo, has strengthened the position of those demanding that Washington try a new approach.

Castro's advancing age is adding to the pressure to break with the current policy. The Cuban leader is now seventy-four. In theory, he could live another decade or two. The odds that he might not, however, have focused attention, both in Cuba and the United States, on the transition issue. For U.S. policymakers, the main goal is to facilitate a peaceful transition to democracy and a market economy. As we have seen, there is considerable disagreement over whether Washington's current policy can achieve that goal. As time passes and Castro continues to age, this debate will undoubtedly intensify.

The visit of Pope John Paul II to Cuba in January 1998 also put pressure on Washington to loosen the embargo in view of Castro's apparent willingness to release some political prisoners and make a number of other concessions regarding the Cuban Catholic Church. Although the Clinton administration rejected calls from a group of Republican senators and former Republican officials, including Henry Kissinger and Senator John Warner, for the establishment of a bipartisan commission to review U.S. policy toward Cuba, Washington implemented a number of new initiatives in January 1999 to increase people-to-people contact between the United States and Cuba. It allowed all U.S. citizens, not just Cuban Americans, to send up to $1,200 annually to any individual or group on the island. It also authorized the sale of some food and agricultural products to independent groups in Cuba. In addition, it authorized an increase in the number of charter flights to Cuba and restored direct mail service to the country.

Within a year after the Pope's visit, however, it became apparent that the Cuban government had decided to increase, rather than decrease, its repression of human-rights groups and political dissidents on the island. As a result, it has become more difficult for critics of U.S. policy to use the Pope's visit to demand further change from Washington.

Until recently, U.S. business groups had remained fairly silent on the Cuba issue. Their behavior began to change in the mid-1990s in reaction to the increasing use of unilateral economic sanctions as a tool of U.S. policy. The issue that most mobilized the U.S. private sector was the so-called D'Amato legislation, introduced in April 1996 by then-Senator Alfonse D'Amato, a Republican of New York. His bill, which punishes foreign companies making large investments in the oil and gas industries of Iran and Libya, was the catalyst for the formation of U.S.A. Engage, a broad coalition of major U.S. multinationals formed to combat the use of U.S. economic sanctions. Although the Cuban embargo was not their primary concern, the anti-embargo movement benefited from having Cuba, which concerned big business far less than Libya or Iran, treated as part of a larger issue. The Clinton administration succeeded in defusing big business's opposition to the Cuban embargo somewhat by relaxing some of the prohibitions that had most angered USA Engage—the sanctions affecting the oil industry's ability to operate in Libya and Iran. Big business was also partially placated by the administration's decision to allow the sale of food and agricultural products to Cuban entities that were independent of the government, as well as the upgrading of telecommunications links with the island. In coming years, the degree of business pressure for a loosening of the embargo against Cuba will probably depend on the success of foreign competitors on the island. If they are earning reasonable profits, the U.S. private sector will increase its pressure against the embargo. If the situation in Cuba continues to deteriorate economically, and perhaps politically as well, U.S. business may decide it is not worth getting more involved with Cuba until the regime changes.

The group that has had the most impact on U.S. policy toward Cuba is the Cuban American population. Its political clout derives from two factors. First, Cuban Americans are concentrated in two states that are fairly important in political terms, Florida and New Jersey. Together, these states account for 40 electoral votes out of 538 in U.S. presidential elections. In addition, Florida and New Jersey together elect 36 representatives of the 435 in the House of Representatives. Second, Cuban Americans have created one of the most powerful and successful lobbies in the United States. The Cuban American National Foundation (CANF) has used its extensive political contacts and financial resources to support the embargo.

The death in November 1997 of Jorge Mas Canosa, the founder and guiding force behind the CANF, has led some observers to conclude that the foundation's best days are behind it. Signs of disunity within the leadership have surfaced. If the CANF no longer has the political clout that it did under Jorge Mas Canosa, the anti-embargo forces will have lost a formidable foe.

The political talent of Jorge Mas Canosa was not the only reason for the CANF's political power. Also important were the opinions of the Cuban American population that supported it. Mas Canosa's generation, composed of people who had personally suffered and left Cuba as a result of the Cuban revolution, had an understandably strong antipathy to Fidel Castro and were united in their desire to see him removed from power. Since they were barred from legally overthrowing him, the maintenance of the U.S. economic embargo against his regime became the foundation's top priority.

Opponents of the embargo argue that the opinions of Cuban Americans are changing and that the younger generation is increasingly questioning the wisdom of the embargo. As late as 1997, however, data from a Florida International University poll of Cuban Americans in Dade County, Florida, and Union City, New Jersey, found that 78 percent want the embargo continued, even though 75 percent say it has not worked well.[9] Although it is possible that Cuban American support for the embargo will decrease in the coming years, it is premature to conclude that the main group of voters who had backed the embargo no longer does so.

Among the U.S. population in general, support for ending the embargo is stronger. According to a May 2000 Gallup Poll, 48 percent of those questioned support ending the trade embargo against Cuba, while 42 percent oppose doing so.[10] In an earlier poll, done in 1994 by Time/CNN, only 35 percent of Americans said the United States should end the embargo, compared with 51 percent who said it should not. The polls are not strictly comparable since they were done by different organizations, but they are indicative of a gradual shift in U.S. public opinion.

On the other hand, there seems to be some confusion among informants regarding U.S. policy toward Cuba. In the 2000 Gallup poll, for example, while 48 percent of those responding favored lifting the embargo, 57 percent of the same sample said they wanted the United States to reestablish diplomatic relations with Cuba. Apparently at least 9 percent of the respondents believed it was possible to maintain the embargo while reestablishing normal diplomatic relations with Cuba, a situation that is a legal contradiction. Furthermore, as is common in public opinion polls, the wording of questions seems to influence the answers received. In the past, when respondents were asked if they favored negotiating with the Castro government, or reestablishing normal diplomatic relations with the Cuban government, many respondents said yes. If the wording were changed to include a description of the Castro government as repressive, dictatorial, or otherwise lacking in political freedom, the positive responses declined. The bottom line is that there is still strong support for the embargo among Cuban Americans, although the U.S. population at large may be less committed to it than ever before.

Without a major change in U.S. public opinion, and in the opinions of Cuban Americans in particular, it is doubtful that the current Congress will approve an end to the embargo. The balance of power between pro- and anti-embargo forces in Congress would change, however, if the Democrats were to regain control of the House of Representatives and the Senate in the near future. Such a development would produce changes in the leadership of key congressional committees. Specifically, if Senator Jesse Helms, a Republican of North Carolina and one of the leading hard-liners toward Cuba, were to be replaced by a proengagement senator as head of the Senate Foreign Relations Committee, a more liberal approach to Cuba might become more likely.

The odds favoring a significant change in U.S. policy toward Cuba would increase dramatically if Cuba were to open up politically. The Helms-Burton bill already provides for a loosening of the embargo if Cuba were to establish a transition government that did not include Fidel or Raúl Castro and was committed to organizing free, fair, and internationally supervised elections. Even short of that, pressure to modify U.S. policy toward Cuba would increase if the Cuban government were to implement reforms that reduced its hold over its labor force. Specifically, if the government were to allow foreign investors to hire and pay workers directly, U.S. business might press for an easing of the embargo. Additional changes such as allowing workers to unionize, permitting independent newspapers, and releasing political prisoners would further strengthen the position of advocates of engagement with the Cuban government.

The fact remains that U.S. attitudes and policy toward Cuba are, and will continue to be, strongly affected by the nature and behavior of the Cuban government. If Castro agrees to some of the changes outlined above, support for ending the embargo would increase. After Castro leaves the scene, it would become even more difficult to keep the embargo in place, although the nature of the post-Castro political system would still influence both Washington's ability and inclination to change its policy toward Cuba.

If the Castro regime were to be replaced by an equally undemocratic system led by Communist Party hard-liners, it is doubtful that Cuban Americans or the U.S. Congress would press hard for a change in U.S. policy. Business interests also would not have much incentive to lobby for an end to the embargo, since the relatively closed Cuban economy would not provide enough new profit-making opportunities to excite them.

If a military-led transitional regime were to follow Castro's departure, opportunities for change would be greater, depending on whether the military promised to limit its tenure in office and prepare the country for open, competitive elections. The more moderate voices within the Cuban American community would be strengthened vis-à-vis the hard-liners, and the U.S. private sector would lobby for increased economic engagement.

If a reformist government were to succeed Castro and further open the economy, additional opportunities for a more proengagement U.S. policy would appear. Key reforms might include the privatization of selected state enterprises, the opening of additional sectors of the economy to foreign investment, and the ability of foreign employers to hire and pay Cuban workers directly. The Cuban American lobby might adopt a less isolationist stance toward the new government. Washington, in turn, might then allow renewed relations between Cuba and international financial institutions and find ways to increase its contacts and cooperation with the new leadership. Without the promise of free and fair elections, however, it would be difficult to overturn Helms-Burton or rescind the embargo.

The best possible scenario, in terms of providing the optimal opportunity for U.S. reengagement with both the Cuban people and the Cuban government, would be for Castro to be replaced by a pro-democracy, pro-market-economy government, ideally by peaceful means. Such a government would take steps to address issues obstructing good relations with the United States. It would move to resolve property claims; open new sectors of the economy to private investment, both foreign and domestic; and hold monitored elections. The United States would be able to declare that Cuba was in transition to democracy and progressively lift restrictions on travel, trade, and investment. Cuban Americans, including the Cuban American

National Foundation, would support such moves and actively pursue business opportunities on the island, as would the U.S. private sector in general. Washington would back loans to Cuba from international financial institutions and activate its own economic-assistance program for the island.

As is apparent from the preceding discussion, there are numerous factors that will influence whether or not the U.S. embargo against Cuba can be sustained. Some are dependent on developments within the United States. Others involve potential changes in Cuba. In the last analysis, the sustainability of the embargo will depend on the interaction between the two. This makes it difficult to predict exactly how long the post–Cold War embargo will remain in place. Barring major changes in Cuban or U.S. politics, it seems reasonable to conclude that the current policy will be sustained at least for the next several years.

Final Thoughts

More than a decade has elapsed since the fall of the Soviet Union. During that time, the U.S. embargo has become considerably more fine-tuned. It now differentiates between the people and the government of Cuba and seeks to level the playing field between them. Specifically, the post–Cold War embargo is trying to strengthen civil society in Cuba by providing resources and information to the Cuban people, while making it difficult for the Castro government to profit economically from a relationship with the United States.

It is still too early to know how successful this approach will be. One of the strengths of the policy, however, is that it is flexible. New ways of engaging and helping the Cuban people can be tried while keeping the embargo against the Castro government in place. A recent study by the Council on Foreign Relations offers a veritable road map of options for deepening U.S. engagement with the Cuban people.[11] It describes a series of steps that can be taken to intensify contacts between the people of the United States and Cuba. It also proposes new initiatives for increasing the exchange of information between the Cuban and U.S. populations, as well as the flow of humanitarian aid to private groups and individuals on the island. With regard to the U.S. private sector, it proposes some limited forms of business activity with Cuba to the extent that such activity primarily benefits the Cuban people rather than their government.

This seems a reasonable, more targeted, and less risky way of dealing with the Castro government than the policy of full engagement advocated by critics of the embargo. It is also more likely to produce a consensus within the United States than a decision to abandon the embargo in favor of a policy that has been tried by others with disappointing results.

Notes

1. For a more detailed discussion of the U.S. embargo see Susan Kaufman Purcell, "Cuba," in Richard N. Haass, ed., *Economic Sanctions and American Diplomacy* (New York: Council on Foreign Relations Press, 1998), pp. 35–56.

2. The U.S. embargo against Cuba prohibits U.S. trade with, and investment in, Cuba. Both U.S. companies and their foreign subsidiaries fall under this prohibition. The embargo also seeks to deprive the Castro government of hard currency it needs for imports by forbidding most U.S. citizens to travel to Cuba. In recent years, the embargo has been loosened in some areas and tightened in others. For a chronology of the evolution of the embargo see Appendix A.

3. Gerardo Trueba González, "Los Efectos del Bloqueo de Estados Unidos en Cuba: Características y Perspectivas," in *Cuba: Apertura Económica y Relaciones con Europa* (Madrid: Instituto de Relaciones Europeo-Latinoamericanas, 1994), p. 84.

4. Edward González, *Cuba: Clearing Perilous Waters?* (Santa Monica: RAND, 1996), p. x.

5. A major foreign investor in Cuba's energy sector is TOTALFINA of France. Important foreign investors in its tourism sector are Sol Melia of Spain and Sherritt of Canada. The BM Group of Israel is a large investor in real estate development in Cuba.

6. Grupo Posadas, Mexico's largest hotel group, is withdrawing from negotiations to acquire two properties in Cuba "from fear of reprisals under the Helms-Burton Act." Cuba*Info* 11, no. 13 (October 5, 1999): 6. Other companies that have decided not to proceed with planned investments after the implementation of Helms-Burton include Domos, a Mexican telecommunications company, and Cemex, a Mexican cement company.

7. The Cuban government recently put a price tag on the cost of the U.S. embargo to Cuba when it announced a new lawsuit against the United States that seeks $100 billion to compensate the Cuban people for the suffering caused by the embargo. In early November 1999, a Cuban court found the U.S. government liable for deaths and damages to Cuba during

forty years of "aggressive policies" and ordered Washington to pay $181 billion in reparations. Cuba*Info* 11, no. 15 (November 23, 1999): 5.

8. Because many nongovernmental groups and organizations are government-infiltrated, some of the resources are ending up in government coffers. This is unfortunate, but the U.S. funds thus diverted are minimal compared to the windfall that the Cuban government would reap from the United States if the embargo were lifted.

9. Linda Robinson, "Cuba: Time to Rethink U.S. Strategy?" Great Decisions 1998, Foreign Policy Association, p. 49.

10. The Gallup Organization website, www.gallup.com/poll/releases/pr0005.asp, May 11, 2000. The 48 percent in favor of lifting the embargo represents a decline of 3 percent from the preceding year's poll, in which 51 percent of those questioned favored lifting the embargo, while the percentage of those who wanted the embargo maintained stayed at 42 percent.

11. Council on Foreign Relations, *U.S.-Cuban Relations in the 21st Century,* Independent Task Force Report (New York: Council on Foreign Relations Press, 1999).

6

A Call for a Post–Cold War Cuba Policy . . . Ten Years After the End of the Cold War

David J. Rothkopf

For a generation of Americans, Cuba loomed large. Indeed, it was more than a country. Cuba was the emblem of a threat and proof that America's foreign policy must contain communism or communism would consume not just distant lands, but also those in our own backyard.

The Cuban Missile Crisis was perhaps the pivotal moment of the Cold War era. It left an indelible mark on the psyches of all Americans, from that of our youthful president who symbolized the promise of the postwar era to those of schoolchildren crouched beneath their desks during air-raid drills. It underscored that the Cold War was only cold on the surface, that unmanaged it could unleash the unthinkable, a nuclear nightmare that would in an instant wipe away not only the U.S.'s dreams but perhaps those of the planet.

It is not surprising, then, that almost four decades later, the Cuban Missile Crisis still resonates with many Americans and continues to influence and shape U.S. foreign policy as has been clear throughout the Elián González media frenzy and its aftermath. The continuing presence of the revolutionary leader of that once-ominous enemy haunts the current scene like a ghost of crises past. While but a shadow of its former self, the specter still evokes powerful feelings and sparks fierce debates.

Nonetheless, with the Cold War now more than a decade past, the ability of that specter to command our attention as it once did is beginning to fade. From many corners of the American public, a consensus is being reached on America's long-standing policy of isolating Fidel Castro's Cuba: it is time for a change.

Foreign policy elites have concluded that "Cuban communism is dead as a potent political force in the Western Hemisphere . . . Containment has succeeded, and the era when it needed to be the organizing principle of U.S. foreign policy toward Cuba has ended."[1] The business community, too, has called for change; after a recent visit to the island, the president of the U.S. Chamber of Commerce said, "It is time to open a new chapter in the relations between the people of the United States and the people of Cuba."[2] Similar sentiments have been heard in the halls of Congress. Recently, conservative Republican Senator John Warner of Virginia stated, "Our goal remains clear—a free, democratic and economically viable Cuba— but I am increasingly concerned that America's current policies may not be proving effective in achieving these goals."[3] Even the U.S. Defense Intelligence Agency, in a 1998 report, found that Cuba no longer poses a threat to our national security.[4]

During the past several decades, most Americans who spoke publicly in favor of changing U.S. policy toward Cuba were voices of the left, those who sympathized with Castro or instinctively opposed sometimes heavy-handed U.S. attempts to influence the political landscape of other nations. But those calling for change today are not radical by any means. They are bastions of the establishment—members of the Council on Foreign Relations, leaders of the business community, dyed-in-the-wool Republican defenders of a strong United States. Yet, despite these calls for change, the alterations that have taken place in U.S. policy to date have been incremental, small steps in the face of the geopolitical sea change that followed the Cold War and transformed the context of relations between Washington and Havana. Indeed, some of the changes of the past several years, notably the 1996 passage of the Helms-Burton legislation tightening the embargo on Cuba, have actually converted policies of embargo and isolation from presidential decrees into law, making them even harder to adjust to changing realities. Having said that, in the wake of the Elián González debate, this tide may be turning. Indeed, that drama may have marked the turning point if not the last stand for the extremists because it established that U.S. public opinion on this matter vacillates from apathy to adjusting the policy to new realities.

The case of Elián González has illustrated that a debate that once turned on the fundamental foreign policy interests of the United States has now become shrill, peripheral, and in many ways terribly sad. A little boy who suffered the loss of his mother saw that trauma compounded as he was turned into a political football by anti-Castro zealots grasping at straws in an effort to keep their political views in the national eye. His father's indisputable right under U.S. and international law to raise his son was discounted by relatives and opportunists who in so doing committed what amounts to just the sort of violation of human rights they had been condemning in Cuba for years, rendering the individual rights of an innocent second to the political ambitions of a powerful elite.

Clearly, we are at an important turning point in our foreign policy toward Cuba. A consensus is emerging, even among those of widely varying political perspectives, that a policy change is required. In order to determine what the new policies ought to be, and when and how they should be implemented, it is important that we begin where all policies should begin. We must reassess our national interests in light of the post–Cold War reality, and reevaluate our policies in light of the effectiveness of those we have employed to date. Only then can conclusions be drawn.

Smaller than Pennsylvania, Larger than Life

Cuba has long occupied more space in the minds of U.S. foreign policy makers than it has on any map. Indeed, at the turn of the century during the Spanish-American War, and then later during the Cold War, Cuba was a central concern of U.S. foreign policy, despite the fact that it is slightly smaller than the state of Pennsylvania and has a population that puts it roughly on a par with the other larger nations of the Caribbean.

To understand the extent to which Cuba's role has been amplified by circumstance and context, it is worth taking a closer look at how Cuba ranks among the nations of the world in terms of several significant measures. Cuba's GDP of U.S.$16.9 billion places it between the slightly larger economies of Slovenia ($19.5 billion) and Oman ($17.2 billion) and the slightly smaller economies of Senegal ($15.6 billion) and Lebanon ($15.2 billion). In terms of geography,

Cuba is smaller than Honduras or Benin and larger than Guatemala. Cuba's population of 11 million resembles that of Zimbabwe (11.1 million) and Burkina Faso (11.5 million). Even Cuba's vaunted military of 6 million troops available for service and 3.6 million troops fit for service[5] ranks behind Taiwan (6.4 million and 4.9 million); Venezuela (6.1 million and 4.4 million); and Uzbekistan (6 million and 4.9 million).

Nonetheless, during the second half of the twentieth century, Fidel Castro and his revolution transformed this small island into what was effectively the forward position of our Cold War enemy, the Soviet Union. Cuba was not seen so much as a nation as it was an agent of the other great superpower. It is because of these strategic magnifiers that Cuba quite naturally grew to occupy a prominent place in the minds of U.S. foreign policy makers.

Cuba remained near the top of our list of international concerns for the best of reasons. It was a threat to U.S. security, a place where a missile launch could minutes later result in the deaths of tens of thousands or more Americans. It was also a self-proclaimed wellspring of revolutionary fervor, a training ground for insurgents, and a source of funding, encouragement, and inspiration for others who would counter the United States and capitalism with communism and allegiance to the Soviet bloc.

Containing communism was the principal mission of U.S. foreign policy during the Cold War period. Thus, containing Cuban communism and countering any moves that might increase the Cuban threat—and by extension the Soviet threat—in the Western Hemisphere were natural objectives for U.S. policymakers. The embargo launched in 1962 to isolate Cuba corresponded to similar efforts to cut off the flow of trade with our other perceived enemies. The military attention paid to Cuba complemented this effort, as did our diplomatic maneuvers to isolate Cuba and counter its initiatives internationally.

With the end of the Cold War, the Cuban threat evaporated. Trade with the Soviet Union ground to a halt and billions of dollars in annual Soviet aid and subsidies dried up, delivering a powerful shock that resulted in the unemployment of hundreds of thousands of Cuban workers and deep systemic blows to the Cuban economy. At the same time, Soviet military aid to Cuba disappeared overnight, and Cuba went from being an extension of superpower might to being the home of an underfunded army deprived not only of its supply chain but also its global mission.

Throughout the 1990s, many nations, recognizing the changed reality of the post–Cold War era, sought to restore their ties with Cuba. Cuba has participated actively in international and regional organizations and has restored full diplomatic relations with every nation in the Western Hemisphere except the United States. Cuba's acceptance into the world community is so pervasive that in the most recent UN vote condemning the U.S. embargo of Cuba, every member but one, Israel, voted with Cuba and against U.S. This is not to say that the United States' interests are, or should be, the same as those of other nations. But the UN vote illustrates how dramatically the world situation has changed and how broad is the international consensus that the Cuban threat has ebbed to insignificance.

If the threat that defined U.S. policy toward Cuba is gone, new questions emerge. What are U.S. national interests with regard to Cuba today? How should these interests shape U.S. policy? And what might Cuba become in the near future? The time has come to set aside the rhetoric, politics, and approaches of a past that is no longer relevant and to revisit U.S. policy toward Cuba from the perspective of our national interests. Such an analysis suggests that the best path toward a freer Cuba—that is, the path that most effectively and directly supports U.S. interests—is one that is free from outmoded ideas and special-interest politics.

U.S. National Interests at the Turn of the Century: Just What Kind of Transition Is Most Important?

U.S. policy currently views a transition within Cuba as the litmus test of whether or not our core national objectives have been achieved. The removal of the communist Castro regime and its replacement with a democratic government is the benchmark set by the Helms-Burton legislation for the normalization of U.S.-Cuban relations. Yet, it is legitimate to consider whether the external transitions that have taken place in the world have obviated the importance of such internal changes. With the Soviet Union gone, Cuba is no longer supported by a rich and powerful patron, is no longer an advance arm of a mighty global military force, and is no longer capable of waging even an ideological guerrilla war because its belief system is so universally rejected and debased. As a result, Cuba no longer has the means to threaten either the United States or its interests in this hemisphere with anything but the rhetoric of an aging leader.

Furthermore, the Castro regime's decision to cling to discredited economic policies has further weakened the country and impeded its ability to restore itself, similar to what has occurred with other former Soviet bloc members such as those in Central Europe. Thus, post–Cold War Cuba is weakened to the point of strategic irrelevance for both political and economic reasons, either of which would be sufficiently debilitating in and of itself.

While it is certainly desirable that Cuba undergoes the transition sought by the Helms-Burton legislation, it should be noted that, without the Soviet threat, Cuba is simply another small undemocratic nation on a long list of such countries. We do not isolate or consider as enemies many such nations, and so, as we consider U.S. policy toward Cuba, we must ask which of our crucial national interests dictates that we give this particular island special status. Are there national interests that make it worthwhile to continue to isolate ourselves from our allies on this issue, to continue to allow Cuba to be an irritant in our relations with other countries in Latin America and the world? Absent the Soviet threat, and absent the likelihood of any other meaningful future threat that could not be countered by the United States in its role as the sole remaining superpower, it is difficult to find any such interest.

Let us consider two questions that may help us arrive at a reasonable conclusion about what U.S. policy toward Cuba ought to be. First, what are the most important U.S. national interests with regard to post–Cold War Cuba? The principal remaining threat Cuba poses to the United States is the potential for refugee flows triggered by economic, political, or social turmoil on the island. Secondarily, the Cuban government might by design or incompetence enable others whose interests are at odds with the United States—be they drug dealers or terrorists—to use the island as a staging area, transshipment point, or training site. While the Castro regime is unlikely to be able to support such groups vigorously given its current economic crisis, it is fair to ask whether or not the Cuban government might do so in the future. In assessing a potential Cuban threat, however, the United States must remember that it no longer needs to view actions against Cuba as invoking the wrath of another greater enemy. Given the disparities in power between the two nations, Cuba cannot mount a credible threat to the United States without the

United States being able to neutralize such a threat very early in its development. Finally, while listing our interests in Cuba, few would argue with the assertion that it is in the U.S. interest for Cuba ultimately to become a democratic, free-market state like all the others in the hemisphere.

Second, if Cuba's impact on U.S. national interests is not significant in security terms, then in what respect does it affect the United States? As mentioned above, the potential for refugee flows is perhaps the most significant impact Cuba has on U.S. interests. However, the key to reducing the threat of major refugee flows is for the Cuban economy to offer sufficient opportunity to resident Cubans that they do not feel compelled to take to the seas and seek entry into the United States. The more robust the Cuban economy, the more likely it is that this threat is reduced. Movement toward democracy and free markets will be helpful in strengthening the economy and preventing refugee flows, but neither the U.S. embargo, nor the collapse of the Soviet Union, nor commercial and social intercourse with other nations have prodded Castro toward major, lasting reforms. (Castro has made some reforms, particularly in response to the collapse of the Soviet Union, but many of these have been abandoned, reversed, or slowed down when the economy has improved. In other words, he is tinkering with the engine and has assiduously avoided contemplating its redesign.) Indeed, it seems likely that we will have to wait for real reform until Castro and his ideologically like-minded successors depart the scene. If that is the case, the United States must weigh the costs of the current policy of embargo against the benefits.

A second, more remote threat to U.S. national interests is that Cuba might be a regional troublemaker, allying itself with others who see taking an anti-U.S. stance to be politically beneficial at home. While this has yet to happen fully, it is possible to conceive in the current situation of a time when a frustrated Castro might forge stronger links with an alienated Hugo Chávez in Venezuela and both might become linked, directly or otherwise, with rebel groups in Colombia and elsewhere in the region. While this is a concern that should be monitored, the key is that once again the best way to reduce the risk of this threat is to reduce the factors that might exacerbate U.S.-Cuba tensions.

Among the costs that must be counted is, first, the alienation of our allies resulting from Helms-Burton. In particular, these allies are offended by the extraterritorial application of U.S. law to enforce U.S. opposition to foreign investment in properties in Cuba that were confiscated from U.S. citizens. U.S.-Cuban relations are a regular irritant and a point of contention with U.S. allies, whether pertaining to U.S. efforts to block Cuban entrance into regional institutions or Cuba's efforts to win global condemnation of our embargo. Second, the embargo places further pressure on the Cuban economy and may lead to just the kind of refugee problem the United States wants to avoid. Third, the United States' current stance of isolating Cuba neatly provides Castro with an enemy to vilify and blame for the economic difficulties of his nation. A final cost is that the policy simply has not worked and is not likely to work in the future, yet it demands considerable attention to maintain and may later be difficult to extricate ourselves from—a president wishing to ease or lift sanctions would require a Congress willing to challenge Helms-Burton.

The benefits of embargo and isolation are that the United States does exert some pressure on Castro, although more pressure falls on the Cuban people. However, this pressure is not enough to produce the outcome we seek and have sought for forty years. In addition, we supposedly send a message to Castro and his colleagues that there is a benefit to pursuing reforms in the form of closer relations with the United States. However, it should be noted that this carrot has been extended for four decades as well. Finally, on the plus side for politicians, the policy supports the desires of a small and arguably influential special-interest group within the United States.

In short, aside from its proximity to the United States, the factors that gave Cuba disproportionate prominence and warranted special, often costly, U.S. policies are gone. The United States has a new set of national interests vis-à-vis Cuba. These include sufficient economic stability to reduce the refugee threat and sufficient political openness to allow greater cooperation on issues ranging from commerce to narcotics control. We also have an interest in opening the way for dialogue that might ultimately advance reform on the island and bring it closer into line with the other countries of the hemisphere. This last point is a telling one. Proponents of maintaining the policy status quo argue that Cuba is a dangerous exception in the hemisphere—the only nondemocracy, the only nation seeking to advance views antithetical to our own. This is simply not the case. In Peru, President Fujimori suspended democracy to suit his own purposes, essentially making himself a new-age *caudillo*. In Paraguay, in the words of one high-ranking Argentine diplomat with whom I spoke, "we are just trying to maintain the appearance of democracy," but it is "in reality, a sham."[6] In Colombia, the democratically elected government controls only a portion of the country, while the threat Colombia poses to the United States as the leading supplier of cocaine and heroin vastly outstrips anything that Cuba could muster. In Venezuela, our largest oil supplier, an old-fashioned military strongman is consolidating power in his hands to the detriment of real pluralism and the democratic institutions of that country. Yet in none of these cases do we consider aggressively isolating these regimes or maintain a legislatively mandated stance requiring a particular political outcome before normal relations are possible.

Why not? Is it that democracy is more important in Cuba than elsewhere in the hemisphere? That the threat posed by a superannuated Castro is greater than that posed by narco-terrorists who profiteer from death in the streets of the United States and who, via transshipment through Mexico, are gradually corrupting and destabilizing a close neighbor of the United States? Obviously, neither position is defensible.

Clearly, the reason the United States avoids policies of isolation toward other countries is that they do not work. We have learned repeatedly that unilateral embargoes or sanctions are ineffective levers and that, by alienating our allies, they may actually reduce our influence and compromise our ability to lead. We also must acknowledge that while engagement may not produce overwhelming results, it at least promotes dialogue. In a post–Cold War world where U.S. influence is diminished, this may be the best we can do.

This analysis of our interests suggests that the United States should seek to recast its policies toward Cuba so that they are viewed principally in the context of our broader policies toward the Caribbean and the Americas and are not seen as sui generis. Cuba is no longer a unique case, except that Castro's regime is communist. But we deal with communist governments in Beijing and Hanoi, with a communist legislature in Moscow, and with other distasteful forms of government from monarchies to dictatorships to kleptocracies on almost every continent. We do not isolate them. Many we even embrace.

Just as current U.S.-Cuban relations evolved within the context of our broader Cold War stance, so should the dominant regional theme of our times—a convergence of hemispheric values and interests—be that which drives U.S.-Cuban relations in the decade ahead. To the extent that Cuba resists such a convergence of values and interests, the United States should consider the use of the tools at its disposal—both carrots and sticks—to promote our interests and to do so in a manner that is commensurate with Cuba's real importance in the region, rather than with the importance it once had. But we must realize that we have precious little influence over the pace of change and the internal politics of the island, as the track record of the embargo shows—and as Castro's failure to initiate real reform in response to the economic catastrophe that followed the fall of the Soviet Union also reflects. Consequently, we must be careful to cast our expectations at the right level, build a policy based on what is achievable, recognize as we have not thus far what is not achievable, and make choices based on this analysis. The choice to preserve and strengthen the embargo sends a strong message, but it will not change Castro, just as it has not changed him in forty years. Our current approach, thanks to the extraterritorial extension of U.S. law under Helms-Burton (to effectively prosecute citizens of governments that happen to have policies that are different from ours . . . which would be virtually every major country in the world) and the tensions caused by clinging to a policy at odds with the rest of the world, continues to have a cost that is greater than its negligible benefits. A new approach is long overdue.

Consequently, the time has come to stop equivocating, postponing, playing politics, ignoring the failures of long-standing policies, and waiting for Higher Powers to take matters into their own hands. The time has come to recognize the failure of the embargo, the failings of Helms-Burton, and to undo the damage done by both. Helms-Burton should be repealed. The embargo should be lifted. The United States should bring its Cuba policy into the new millennium.

There are many compelling reasons for ending the embargo immediately, not least of which is that it does not work. Ending the embargo now would remove an important arrow from Castro's quiver by undemonizing the United States and by showing that we want better relations with the Cuban people. Ending the embargo now would reduce the risk of further economic pressures that could increase the likelihood of future refugee crises or transitional instability on the island. Ending the embargo now would reduce tension with our allies in the Western Hemisphere and elsewhere, and underscore that the

United States is prepared to lead within the international institutions we have created. Above all, we should end the embargo now because the rationale that lay behind it has been consigned to the pages of history. Our future with a new Cuba will only be enhanced by dialogue. This is especially true in a world in which we can always quickly and fairly easily revert to forceful expressions of our interest because we are the world's sole remaining superpower and will forever be vastly more powerful than our tiny island neighbor.

Once the embargo is ended, the carrots we can use to achieve our objectives can and should be those we use elsewhere. These could include limited flows of aid dollars to support organizations that enable the development of pluralism in Cuba, action in multilateral forums that promote democracy and free markets, and support of efforts by the church and other nongovernmental organizations that help our view. And we must realize that withholding these carrots is the best stick we can use, beyond public condemnation and diplomatic pressure in suitable venues. In short, we must also realize that in the end what we can do is quite limited and that we should make the great and sometimes difficult leap for U.S. policymakers of accepting this fact.

Furthermore, our policy should seek to promote Cuban reform as much because the current system is likely to be unstable as it is because it is ideologically antithetical to our views. The ideological issues that were once central to Cold War policies are less important than the perspective that our principal national interest is in a stable Cuba. Specifically this means not setting policy bars that are linked purely to ideological objectives as in Helms-Burton, or linking policies to whether or not Castro is in power (another vestige of a historic stance), and rather focusing on and accepting the idea of much more gradual changes. These will raise Cuban hopes and enhance Cuban stability. This approach—the alternative to waiting for total ideological victory—is not only better linked to our real national interests but will give us more influence in the formative reform years. Under the current approach, it is possible for Helms-Burton to remain in place even in the event of significant economic reforms in Cuba, even some important political reforms. Extensive political, social, economic, and cultural interchange between the United States and the island is far more likely than the current policy to lead to a better understanding among Cubans of our views and interests. An understanding of the merits of our system, along with Cuba's economic success, is more likely to lead to demands for a pluralistic system than any of the approaches recently employed by the United States. This is, in fact, the engagement approach that we have chosen in China and elsewhere. It is an approach based on the simple principle that the United States can do more to foment change by remaining involved with a country, by having a presence there, than by walking away. It recognizes the universally acknowledged shortcomings of unilateral embargo in a world in which U.S. trade accounts for less than 15 percent of total trade and many others are willing to step in. This approach acknowledges that an exchange of products and services brings with it an exchange of ideas and ideals to draw a country into the new global economy and require openness to achieve competitiveness. It employs common sense rather than inflammatory rhetoric to protect U.S. interests. There is no reason why Cuba should be treated differently or why Cuba warrants the high international costs that result from our current policy. (And we should note that, as the embargo does not work but carries a cost, even if engagement fails but has no similar cost or offers secondary benefits with regard to our other international relations, it is thus the superior policy choice.)

Another way to view this assessment of policy alternatives is to observe that since the embargo is demonstrably ineffective in Cuba, it can have value only as a symbol. And this value must be calculated against the costs it incurs. One such cost of the embargo, which deprives the Cuban economy of $1 billion a year according to Andrew Zimbalist, is the pain it visits on the innocent. Those who suffer are not the leaders who remain resolutely in power and undeniably well fed. Furthermore, should Cuba collapse soon or Castro depart of natural causes and the embargo end, it is virtually certain that the United States will quickly find itself in the position of having to spend as much as $6 billion per year to help rebuild the Cuban economy. As in Haiti, the contribution required of the United States will be greater thanks to an embargo that ultimately failed to advance our interests in any measurable way.

The failure of the embargo has been exacerbated in recent years by the Helms-Burton bill, legislation that many critics have noted tramples on international legal principles long championed by the United States through its extraterritorial provisions, alienates our closest allies, and does little to advance U.S. interests. Helms-Burton is the product of a combination of two pernicious Washington impulses. The first is the impulse, already noted, to fight the last war. The second is a desire to pander to a politically relevant special-interest group—in this case, Cuban exiles in the politically important states of Florida and New Jersey.

Politics and Policy

Any analysis of U.S. foreign policy toward Cuba must inevitably touch upon domestic politics. When one observes the differences between how we treat Cuba and how we treat other nations that were even greater Cold War enemies, or why we treat a little boy like Elián González differently than we would treat any other little boy from any other land in the same circumstances, the question arises as to why. The analysis of policy options conducted above suggests that the policies we have chosen to date are not in our best interests. And, again, we must ask why.

The answer, as even defenders of the status quo will acknowledge, is that U.S. policy toward Cuba is largely not a foreign policy issue at all. Rather it is an issue of U.S. domestic politics resulting from a carefully managed campaign by the community of Cuban Americans who were dispossessed by Castro, to keep pressure on him until their personal scores are settled. (The personal dimension of the policy is illustrated by the fact that the Helms-Burton bill, which is intended to support our national security by isolating Cuba, gives individual U.S. citizens with claims in Cuba the right to waive the bill's provisions in the event they reach a satisfactory settlement for their disputed property in Cuba. This may be the only instance in U.S. history when individuals can independently waive U.S. national-security interests for the right price.)

Interestingly, however, several misconceptions exist about the nature of the Cuban American lobby in the United States. Clearly, it is powerful. The Cuban American National Foundation and large Cuban American–owned companies have made political donations to influential policymakers like Senator Jesse Helms (chairman of the Senate Foreign Relations Committee) and others. These, coupled with the role of Cuban Americans in the politics of New Jersey and

Florida, both strong states electorally with fifteen and twenty-five electoral votes respectively, have been powerful levers in initiating and maintaining policies like the embargo and the Helms-Burton bill.

But it may be not only that the power of this group is overstated, but also that its views are beginning to change. To understand this, one need only look to electoral statistics. In 1996, Cuban American voters made up 7 percent, or 371,000, of the 5.3 million voters in Florida who actually exercised their right to vote.[7] This might seem like a fairly substantial number, as only 300,000 votes separated Bill Clinton's 2,545,968 votes from Bob Dole's 2,243,324 in the 1996 presidential election. Historically, from the mid-1960s to the mid-1990s, on average almost 85 percent of Florida's Cuban Americans voted for Republicans. This deep loyalty to a single party suggests that the idea of Democratic candidates courting the Cuban vote might bring limited returns. Nonetheless, a swing has taken place toward the Democratic Party during the past decade. Whereas Michael Dukakis won only 15 percent of the Cuban American vote in Florida in 1988, Bill Clinton won 22 percent in 1992. In 1996, Clinton, who had by then signed the Helms-Burton bill and was viewed as more sympathetic to Cuban issues, won 34 percent of the Cuban American vote. Thus, between 1988 and 1996, the Democratic candidate had increased his share of the Cuban American vote by 19 percentage points. The question is whether this gain—amounting to a total of 70,000 votes, or about 1.5 percent of the total Florida vote—was due to the increasingly hard-line policy stance taken by the Democratic candidate or other factors.

Even though Clinton's stance was tougher than that of, say, Dukakis in 1988, data suggests that many of these 70,000 votes were won not because of the change in policy but as a consequence of a generational shift taking place within the Cuban American community. Younger Cuban Americans are less emotionally invested in the anti-Castro politics of the past. Older Cuban American voters are starting to care more about issues like health care and retirement benefits (on which Democrats are strong) than they do about issues that held them in thrall in the past. This is a gradual process. A recent study published by Florida International University (FIU) reveals that, of the one in four Cuban Americans born in the United States, 40 percent say they are predisposed toward being Democrats.[8] Of those Cuban Americans who emigrated when they were aged ten or younger, 26.7 percent view themselves as Democrats.

Thus, a substantial portion of the approximately 70,000 votes picked up by Clinton may have been the result of these shifts.[9] Consequently, the swing to Clinton that can be attributed to something other than party affiliation or this generational shift is about 57,000, just over one percent of the Florida presidential vote in 1996, or 18.8 percent of Clinton's winning margin in Florida. This suggests that in Florida, the state said to drive U.S. policy because of the influence of Cuban voters, the gains from taking a hard-line policy stance did not have a pivotal effect on the outcome of the presidential election. (It is also worth noting that the FIU study concluded that where the respondents were born and how much of their lives were spent in the United States were a much better indicator of how they voted than their self-professed ideology.) Some might say that such an outcome is not a bad gain politically, but it is worth understanding the stakes—fewer than 60,000 votes in a nation of almost 300 million are driving a policy of questionable merit and with significant drawbacks. (State politics obviously do have a greater effect on state elections and therefore strongly Cuban American districts do tend to produce more hard-line anti-Castro representatives, whose jobs depend much more on satisfying this group.)

Furthermore, it is important to note that the results of the FIU study shed additional light on where these voters stand on U.S.-Cuba policy. While the study notes that a substantial majority of all Cuban Americans still favor the status quo in U.S. policy toward Cuba, this opinion is held most strongly by those who came to the United States when older than eleven, with 73.4 percent favoring holding the line. Among those who came under the age of ten, only 58.9 percent favor withholding recognition of the Cuban government, with 64.1 percent of Cuban Americans born in this country favoring this position. The FIU study concludes:

> The results . . . hint at the possibility that Cuban American politics is becoming less monolithic. The political cohesiveness which characterized the first generation of exile politics may be giving way to more diversity. As the inexorable march of time and the inevitable toll it takes on human mortality continues, one would logically expect Cuban American attitudes in the aggregate to mirror those attitudes seen in the younger generations of this analysis.[10]

Some who oppose the idea of simply lifting the embargo believe that, while such a move may be desirable, it is unrealistic politically.

The facts suggest otherwise. The strategy of supporting the embargo to win an electoral advantage seems to fall into the category of wishful thinking, as factors such as age and party affiliation appear to carry far more weight than policy stances in determining political outcomes. Just as time will ensure that the Cold War realities that led to the current policies of embargo and isolation recede into memory, so will the "monolithic" Cuban American voting bloc that was a key justification for supporting such policies even after the security rationale for them had long since disappeared.

Engage, Normalize, and Prepare for Threats

Many argue that the reason to maintain current U.S. policy toward Cuba is to keep the pressure on Castro until he steps down. But it is legitimate to ask what such a strategy achieves beyond a possible moral victory. Who gains? Who suffers? Some Cuba observers in the study group that led to the publication of this book point out that it is Castro himself who benefits from the embargo because it allows him to gain stature as a feisty David facing a capitalist Goliath ninety miles away. Evidence also suggests that it is the people of Cuba who suffer, as the embargo weakens the Cuban government's ability to deal with the nation's social needs and enhances the likelihood of future economic difficulties. Ironically, keeping the pressure on may actually increase the chances that a refugee crisis—the one near-term threat actually posed by the island—will come to pass.

Others argue that Castro is so ruthless and bloodthirsty that the United States simply cannot deal with him. This is inconsistent with the reality of U.S. foreign policy elsewhere. The United States deals all the time with governments that are just as ruthless and ideologically at odds with us as Cuba, governments representing people who have far less in common with us, governments representing interests far more threatening to us, from the monarchies of the Persian Gulf to the Central Committee in Beijing. In recent years, we have coddled dictators like Indonesia's Suharto, who was both stunningly corrupt and responsible for a genocide in East Timor, and the post-Soviet successor government in Moscow, with its communist-controlled Duma, its dysfunctional and corrupt institutions, and its reckless disregard for civilian casualties in Chechnya.

A reappraisal of Cuba from the perspective of U.S. interests at the dawn of the twenty-first century yields the following conclusions:

- Cuba is not a geopolitical threat to the United States.
- Cuba could become a threat to the United States in terms of refugee flows should its economic disintegration continue.
- Cuba's importance to the United States beyond the issue of refugees is economic and symbolic. Economically, Cuba represents a small but attractive potential tourist haven close to our shores. Symbolically, our primary concern is with the absence of democracy on the island.
- The best way to promote stability in Cuba is to encourage a level of economic growth that is sufficient to avoid social meltdown on the island.
- The best way to promote our economic interests in Cuba is to give U.S. companies the chance to invest and compete in the Cuban market.
- The best way to promote democracy in Cuba is to give the Cuban people free and easy access to U.S. ideas and ideals through active engagement with us commercially, culturally, and socially.

Some property issues remain to be dealt with on behalf of dispossessed Cubans living in the United States. These should be handled via the system of international law we helped develop in the post–World War II years. These issues may be thorny, but, taken as a whole, contested assets valued—even by one Cuban American National Foundation (CANF) board member with whom I spoke—at several billion dollars are not of material consequence to a $6 trillion U.S. economy. Moreover, this dispute is not significant enough to warrant punishing the entire Cuban population, alienating the other nations of the hemisphere, and creating tension with our key allies.

Despite the strong rationale for an immediate end to the embargo, given our stance of the past three decades, some might suggest that it would be a politically awkward reversal just to abandon our past policies and begin engagement. It may be more realistic to announce our intention, given the post–Cold War reality, to begin such a process of engagement and initiate a formal dialogue with the island's government in order to achieve it. Along the way, clear goals should be established and made public, and new openings in the relationship should follow from each stage of its development. The objective should be to normalize the U.S.-Cuban relationship as quickly as possible. It is only through normalization that the United States can most quickly achieve our goals and remove this needless irritant from our list of global concerns.

Central to this approach is an idea that may be anathema to some. It is that we should not make normal relations with Cuba contingent on the actual achievement of democracy in that country, any more than we have made normal relations with China, Saudi Arabia, Indonesia, or Mexico contingent on whether those countries have democracies—real or nominal—in place. Democracy is an important goal. However, we have learned that we cannot impose democracy on the island through embargo, and we have concluded that engagement is the best means of promoting democracy elsewhere in the world. The inconsistency between our policy toward Cuba and our policy toward other distasteful regimes is obvious and oft-repeated, and should be corrected as soon as possible. (Foreign policy need not be consistent, but since inconsistency becomes a target for opponents, it must be justifiable and "worth the fight." That is no longer the case with our Cuba policy.)

Focal Points for a New Policy

The new U.S. policy toward Cuba should focus on promoting our interests as directly as possible. For example, if our interest is in promoting stability and avoiding refugee outflows, we should work to find acceptable ways to increase U.S. investment in Cuba and improve the Cuban economy. We should also work toward promoting a smooth transition of power from Fidel Castro to his successor, to the extent we can influence such events. (The economic pressures resulting from the embargo may make an abrupt transition more likely, which is actually contrary to our primary desire of avoiding refugee flows. Consequently, taking a more gradualist approach, offering carrots with each stage of reform, offering technical assistance where it might be accepted, and taking a public stance that does not give fodder to anti-U.S. demagogues in the party hierarchy in Cuba would all help in this regard.) While trying to avoid rewarding the current regime in Cuba, we must accept that money is fungible and that this will be possible only in a limited degree.

Also in light of our interest in promoting Cuban stability and long-term U.S.-Cuban amity, as well as our broader interests in the Caribbean, we should actively begin preparing now for the kind of emergency economic intervention that might be needed in the event of the collapse of the Castro regime or its successor. The ability to step in swiftly with the right programs that bring swift, visible results and build political support for our objectives is key. Days or weeks of hesitation could produce a refugee crisis or worse. Consequently, such contingencies need to be addressed now.

Immediate, active integration of Cuba into the regional institutions of the Americas will promote the adoption of international standards and values by Cuba and will serve to promote Cuba's ties to the Americas economically. This is precisely the same rationale cited by the Clinton administration in its arguments for encouraging Chinese entry into the World Trade Organization (WTO). We need to remember that, in a post-Castro era, our concerns with Cuba will be primarily economic and will remain fairly limited. Nonetheless, one important goal will be to undo the damage done to the U.S. business community by the embargo, which has given European investors an enormous advantage in an island just off our shores.

Future threats from Cuba are likely to arise in areas such as drug smuggling or illegal immigration, and thus it is important that as early as possible close cooperation be established between U.S. and Cuban law enforcement authorities, immigration authorities, customs authorities, and others. Active inclusion of Cuba in regional programs in these areas and expansion of existing programs are also likely to be key focal points of future efforts. Recent progress in pilot efforts in this area should be seen as even stronger evidence of the merits of such approaches.

The fallacy around which current U.S. policy is built is that, short of force, we have no means to promote the removal of the Castro regime from power. The absence of support from any other country makes the task even more insurmountable. Indeed, most experts conclude that transition in Cuba will not come until Castro dies but that thereafter such transition is likely even if a brief stay in power by Fidel's brother Raúl is a consequence of his death. (Raúl is viewed as being in ill health and considerably weaker than his brother.) In the meantime, U.S. policy is being held hostage to the personal animus of a few individuals over an old and now largely irrelevant fight. We do not have a "Cuban Democracy Act"; we have a "Wait Until Fidel Dies Act."

It is time to realize that the United States' greatest influence on Cuba will come from letting the Cuban people experience the benefits of capitalism and democracy. It is time to trust that, via such exposure and given the enormous pressures of world historical trends, the Cubans will change their system by one means or another. The United States should be ready to promote and assist that change and respond to its likely consequences, and then get on with the business of treating Cuba like any other large Caribbean island with which it has relations and from which comes a large immigrant population. The United States should gain what it can from exchanges with Cuban society and from commercial opportunities on the island. We should try to reduce the risks that come from having a poor nation on our doorstep.

The real problem for U.S. policy may be that Cuba has become so comparatively unimportant that the failure of U.S. policies there has had only a limited impact in the United States. This is also fortunate. And it contains an important message. Cuba is not a foreign policy problem for the United States. It is a domestic political problem. If politicians feel that more is to be gained by pandering to special interests than is to be lost by having an ineffective and obsolete policy, then they will continue to pander.

A final useful lesson might be drawn from imagining what would happen if different policies were in place. First, the United States would not have alienated its allies. Second, the United States would not have punished the Cuban people more harshly than their own government. Third, the United States would not have forced U.S. businesses to lose ground to their global competitors. Fourth, the United States would not have exerted tremendous effort on behalf of a policy that has yielded no political change.

It is therefore possible to conclude that having had no policy at all would have served the United States better than our current policy. We should start from there. Undo the damage. Eliminate the embargo. Then introduce whatever measures are most likely to advance U.S. interests. Such a shift will require a sea change in the U.S. approach to Cuba. The fact that the world has changed dramatically since the current policy was initiated suggests the time for that change has come.

Notes

1. Council on Foreign Relations, *U.S.-Cuban Relations in the 21st Century,* Independent Task Force Report (New York: Council on Foreign Relations Press, 1999), p. 2.

2. Statement by Thomas J. Donohue, president and chief executive officer, U.S. Chamber of Commerce, July 16, 1999.

3. Warner, John. "Trade Sanctions Haven't Worked: Time to Sell Food and Medicine to Cuba," *The Virginion-Pilot,* July 16, 1999.

4. Council on Foreign Relations, op. cit., p. 2.

5. The "available for service" figure includes men and women, reserves and active forces, combatants and noncombatants, and thus is not generally considered a very useful gauge of strength.

6. Author's conversation with Argentine diplomat.

7. These electoral statistics come from "Troubled Waters," *Newsweek,* March 11, 1996.

8. Dario Moreno, "The Political Attitude of Young Cubans," Florida International University, online at www.fiu.edu/~morenod/scholar/young.htm.

9. If, as in the Florida International University study, only 10 percent of Cuban American voters were born in the United States and only 10 percent were aged ten or younger when they arrived in the United States, that constitutes a group of 74,000 voters, of whom almost 25,000 view themselves as Democrats. If 15 percent of the 80 percent of other voters view themselves as Democrats (as they have done historically), that would mean another approximately 44,000 votes. By applying Moreno's data to the electoral results provided by the state of Florida, it appears that 69,000 Cuban American voters view themselves as Democrats—more than half of the approximately 126,000 Cuban American votes won by Clinton.

10. Moreno, "Political Attitude."

7

Conclusion:
Cuba's Dilemma, and Ours

William M. LeoGrande

Speculating about what will happen in Cuba when Fidel Castro finally passes from the scene is a perennial parlor game in Washington, D.C., not to mention in Miami. Although the pace of change in Cuba may depend upon the timing of a leadership transition, the dynamics of change are increasingly visible and inexorable. Cuba already confronts the need to adjust to an international environment hostile to centrally planned economies. As it faces this new reality, Cuba's dilemma is whether it can find some way to survive, adjust, and eventually prosper, while at the same time retaining the "achievements" of the revolution.

What constitutes those achievements is itself a matter of contention. Is the essence of the revolution socialism, or simply social welfare? Is it enough to retain the universal health care and educational benefits that are, almost all Cubans agree, the proudest achievements of the revolution? Or must the state retain ownership of at least the commanding heights of the Cuban economy? Moreover, what would state ownership mean, in practice, if the global economy forced the Cuban state to manage its enterprises under the discipline of the market? Key enterprises in external sectors of the Cuban economy, such as tourism, already operate on market principles even though technically they remain state property.

If Cuban socialism succumbs to the exigencies of global capitalism, will the new economy be able to afford social welfare? Even now the government faces severe fiscal imbalances because for so long Cuba lived beyond its means, supported by Soviet subsidies. The experience of other small underdeveloped countries like Costa Rica suggests that comprehensive social programs are very difficult to finance. Perhaps the best scenario one can hope for would be a "soft landing" of the sort recommended by Manuel Pastor Jr.—a program of gradually deepening economic reforms that attempts to preserve maximum social equality. The foremost obstacle to this course of action is political—the unwillingness of Fidel Castro to accept the idea that his socialist experiment has failed.

But whether Castro's passing would unlock that particular log-jam is uncertain. Because Cuba's political system remains closed, it is difficult to know what debates go on within the regime's inner sanctum. Indeed, in the shadow of Castro's dominance, even the debates that do occur probably express a narrower range of views than they would otherwise. In both China after Mao Tse-Tung and the Soviet Union after Stalin, pent-up pressures for change within the political elite led to significant policy shifts. On the other hand, Jaime Suchlicki may be right that conservative forces within the Cuban elite have the strength and determination to stay the course even after Fidel.

For the past forty years, understanding the interior politics of the Cuban regime has been sufficient for understanding Cuban politics. That is becoming less and less true. The skills of a well-trained kremlinologist still have value in analyzing Cuban politics, but the importance of politics outside the regime is growing. Political stirrings outside the boundaries of state-directed institutions and beyond their immediate control point the way toward Cuba's future.

For the most part, the government has been unremittingly hostile to any political reform. As Castro has been forced to make economic concessions to the market, he has held tight to Leninist orthodoxy in politics. No doubt he learned the lesson of Eastern Europe's reform communists, who liberalized in hopes of promoting economic change, only to be swept away in a tide of mass popular rejection. Instead, Castro has chosen the Chinese model of maintaining strict political control during a period of disruptive economic adjustment. Whether this strategy is viable remains an open question, both in China and in Cuba.

As market reforms weaken the Cuban state's control over the economy, its political monopoly has become frayed as well. Emergent entrepreneurs, both farmers and small-businesspeople, depend less and less on the state for their well-being. As they accumulate wealth and grow increasingly indispensable to the health of the economy, their desire for less government interference, regulation, and taxation is certain to take a more explicitly political direction. As Cubans increasingly interact with populations abroad, through tourism, family visits, and professional cooperation (all of which the government promotes for economic reasons), the danger of "ideological contamination" increases. And as the legitimacy of the regime erodes because of the failure of Cuba's socialist model, ordinary Cubans are bound to ask (as Cuban intellectuals already do) whether there should not be more open debate about alternative futures. The growth of the Catholic Church is an important indicator of the loss of revolutionary spirit and the popular hunger for an alternative. The government can continue to try to quell these stirrings, but it cannot eliminate them because they are the unavoidable by-product of the economic concessions to capitalism Cuba has been forced to make. The government's rapprochement with the church is a bellwether accommodation because it represents the surrender of the regime's ideological and organizational monopoly.

As Susan Kaufman Purcell points out, it would be wrong to think that these dynamics lead deterministically toward a democratic transition. Where they will lead depends on the complex interaction of several key factors, including the pace of economic change, elite tolerance for independent associations that are (initially at least) nonadversarial, the role of the church, and the ability of the Cuban regime to retain some measure of popular legitimacy (through improved economic performance, nationalist appeals, or unifying confrontations with foreign adversaries over issues like the custody of Elián González). All of these are inherently unpredictable. But the reinsertion of Cuba into the global economy has set in motion internal economic processes that are corroding the regime's monopoly on power. For the first time in forty years, politics outside the regime are at least as interesting and portentous as politics inside it.

Our Dilemma

Washington's dilemma is how to promote peaceful change in Cuba, or—perhaps more honestly—how to avoid a violent denouement, which almost everyone agrees would be a threat to U.S. interests.

The contemporary debate over U.S. policy turns in large part on disagreements over what actions are most likely to have the desired effect, and on this, reasonable people can disagree, as this volume demonstrates.

Underlying these divergent policy recommendations are disagreements over the dynamics of change within Cuba itself. Observers who believe that Fidel Castro remains firmly in control, that he can weather the current economic crisis with minimal reforms, and that he can manage the political fallout, will conclude that the Cuban regime is stable and will not change of its own volition. External pressure is then a logical strategy to disrupt the regime's equilibrium and hasten change. This argument has two major weaknesses: first, external pressure has not forced significant change in the regime thus far, and unilateral economic sanctions (Washington's main weapon against Castro) are notoriously ineffective. Second, if this strategy succeeds too well, it could produce the violent collapse that Washington is most anxious to avoid.

Alternatively, observers who believe that the economic changes under way in Cuba are substantial and irreversible, that they have significant political implications, and that they might accelerate under favorable international conditions will conclude that a policy of engagement makes the most sense. The key weakness of this approach is also its poor track record. As pursued by Western Europe and Canada since the fall of the Soviet Union, it has not yet produced any significant political change. If the underlying assumptions of a policy of engagement prove mistaken, it is not likely to increase the probability of a violent end to the Cuban regime, but it might well increase its longevity.

The future of Cuban politics is uncertain, and so, therefore, is U.S. policy. The downside risk of the policy of hostility is that it may produce violence and chaos, rather than peaceful change. The downside risk of the policy of engagement is that it may prolong Cuba's authoritarian system rather than liberalizing it. Advocates line up based largely on which of these risks they are more willing to take.

One thing is certain: the future will draw Cuba and the United States closer together. By prioritizing tourism as the growth sector of the new Cuban economy, even Fidel Castro implicitly acknowledges that reconciliation with the United States—the source of most Caribbean tourists—is inevitable. The forces that historically linked

Cuba and the United States so intimately—geography and economic complementarity—will be reinforced in the future by the Cuban American community. Already, their travel and remittances have become a major source of hard currency for the island. When political barriers between the two countries come down, Cuban Americans will be a natural bridge, providing the island with much-needed foreign investment, managerial skill, and entrée to U.S. markets. There is also a risk that they might return to buy up the island's productive assets, creating a dominant class of expatriates, thereby sowing the seeds for future instability. Or they might try to use their wealth as leverage to control Cuban politics once a democratic transition eventually gets under way. In short, the reunification of the Cuban family could be an occasion for recrimination and bitterness as well as joy. Cubans, no less than Salvadorans and Guatemalans, must make a conscious decision to seek reconciliation and look ahead toward cooperation rather than backward toward the settling of accounts. When they do, the long winter of U.S.-Cuban relations may finally give way to spring.

Appendix A

Chronology of the
U.S. Embargo Against Cuba

Sept. 4, 1961   The U.S. Congress passes the Foreign Assistance Act
                 of 1961, prohibiting aid to Cuba and authorizing the
                 president to establish and maintain "a total embargo
                 upon all trade between the United States and Cuba."

Feb. 7, 1962   President John F. Kennedy declares an embargo on
                 all trade with Cuba. The U.S. government also pro-
                 hibits all Cuban imports and the re-export of U.S.
                 products to Cuba from other countries.

Aug. 1, 1962   The U.S. Congress amends the Foreign Assistance
                 Act to prohibit U.S. aid "to any country which fur-
                 nishes assistance to the present government in
                 Cuba."

Oct. 2, 1962   U.S. ports are closed to nations that allow their
                 ships to carry arms to Cuba; ships that have docked
                 in a socialist country are prohibited from docking in
                 the United States during that voyage; and the trans-
                 port of U.S. goods is banned on ships owned by
                 companies that trade with Cuba.

Feb. 8, 1963   The Kennedy administration prohibits travel to
                 Cuba by U.S. citizens and makes financial and
                 commercial transactions with Cuba illegal for U.S.
                 citizens.

May 14, 1963   The U.S. Department of Commerce requires specific
                 approval for exports of food and medicines to Cuba.

133

Dec. 1963   The U.S. Congress amends the Foreign Assistance
                 Act to prohibit U.S. aid to countries that fail to take
                 steps to prevent aircraft or ships under their registry
                 from engaging in trade with Cuba.

1975   The Ford administration eases restrictions on ex-
                 ports to Cuba by foreign subsidiaries of American
                 companies; the U.S. government also relaxes its pro-
                 hibition against third-country exports to Cuba that
                 contain U.S.-origin parts, allowing such countries to
                 request licenses to export goods containing up to 20
                 percent of such parts. The denial of aid to third
                 countries that permit their ships to trade with Cuba
                 is also revoked. Direct trade remains embargoed.

Mar. 18, 1977   The Carter administration lifts the prohibition on
                 travel to Cuba and allows U.S. citizens to spend
                 $100 on Cuban goods during their visits.

1978   The U.S. Treasury regulations are changed to allow
                 U.S. residents to send money to relatives in Cuba.

Apr. 9, 1982   The Reagan administration halts charter air links
                 between Miami and Havana.

Apr. 19, 1982   The Reagan administration prohibits monetary ex-
                 penditures in Cuba by U.S. citizens, with the excep-
                 tion of a narrowly defined group of professionals,
                 thereby effectively banning travel to the island.

Nov. 20, 1989   The U.S. Department of the Treasury sets travel-
                 related expenses for U.S. citizens to Cuba at $100
                 per day.

Oct. 15, 1992   Congress passes the Cuban Democracy Act, infor-
                 mally known as the Torricelli bill, which prohibits
                 foreign-based subsidiaries of U.S. companies from
                 trading with Cuba, travel to Cuba by U.S. citizens,
                 and family remittances to Cuba. The law allows pri-
                 vate groups to send food and medicine to Cuba. The
                 law also prohibits ships entering Cuban ports for
                 purposes of trade from loading and unloading
                 freight in the United States for 180 days. It more
                 tightly restricts the kinds of U.S. citizens who can
                 spend money in Cuba without special permission
                 from the U.S. Treasury, and requires those seeking
                 to send remittances to the island to get licenses

from the Treasury's Office of Foreign Assets Control. It authorizes, but does not require, the president to declare any country providing assistance to Cuba ineligible for aid under the Foreign Assistance Act of 1961, ineligible for assistance or sales under the Arms Export Control Act, and ineligible under any program providing for the forgiveness or reduction of debt owed to the U.S. government. It also allows the president to waive the prohibitions on foreign-subsidiary trade or the restrictions on third-country vessels trading with Cuba if and when he determines that the Cuban government has held free, fair, and internationally supervised elections; has allowed opposition parties sufficient time to organize and campaign, and has given them full access to the media; is showing respect for civil liberties and human rights; and is moving toward the establishment of a market economy. It also encourages an increase in contact and communication with nongovernment groups and individuals on the island via telecommunications, visits by authorized U.S. travelers, and the like.

Oct. 5, 1995   President Clinton announces measures to expand people-to-people contacts between the United States and Cuba, to allow U.S. nongovernmental organizations to fund projects in Cuba, and to provide AID funding to U.S. nongovernmental organizations for Cuba-related projects.

Mar. 12, 1996   Following the shoot-down by the Cuban military of two private U.S. planes piloted by members of Brothers to the Rescue, President Clinton signs the Cuban Liberty and Democratic Solidarity (Libertad) Act, or the so-called Helms-Burton bill. Title I of the act strengthens sanctions against the incumbent Cuban government. Among many other provisions, it codifies (transforms into law) the U.S. embargo on trade and financial transactions, which had been in effect pursuant to a presidential proclamation since the Kennedy administration. Title II describes U.S. policy toward and assistance to a free and

independent Cuba. It requires the president to produce a plan for providing economic assistance to a
transitional or democratic government in Cuba. Title
III creates a private cause of action and authorizes
U.S. nationals with claims to confiscated property in
Cuba (including those who were Cuban citizens at
the time of the confiscation) to file suit in U.S.
courts against persons who may be "trafficking" in
that property. The act grants the president the authority to suspend the lawsuit provisions of Title III
for periods of six months at a time if he deems it is
necessary to the national interest of the United
States and will expedite a transition to democracy in
Cuba. Title IV requires the denial of visas to, and
exclusion from the United States of, persons who,
after March 12, 1996, confiscate or "traffic" in confiscated property in Cuba claimed by U.S. nationals.

July 16, 1996   President Clinton suspends enforcement of Title III
provisions of the Helms-Burton bill, which permit
suits to be filed in U.S. courts against foreign investors who are trafficking in U.S.-claimed confiscated property.

Jan. 3, 1997   President Clinton again suspends Title III of the
Helms-Burton bill.

Feb. 12, 1997   President Clinton approves licenses for U.S. news
organizations to open bureaus in Cuba. Only CNN
is allowed in by the Cuban government.

July 16, 1997   President Clinton for the third time suspends Title
III of the Helms-Burton bill.

Jan. 1998   President Clinton again suspends Title III of the
Helms-Burton bill.

Mar. 20, 1998   Existing U.S. regulations regarding Cuba are
amended as follows:

- U.S. citizens may send up to $,1200 annually to
relatives in Cuba.
- Direct passenger flights between Cuba and the
United States are permitted.
- Travel is banned if it is not for humanitarian purposes or professional research or related to the
sales of pharmaceutical and medical goods. U.S.

	travelers are not allowed to spend more than $100 per day in Cuba.
July 16, 1998	President Clinton again suspends Title III of the Helms-Burton bill.
Jan. 1999	The Clinton administration announces the following changes in the embargo:

- It relaxes the rules on sending money to Cuba so that anyone in the United States may send up to $1,200 annually to any individual or group in Cuba, with the exception of high-ranking Cuban government officials. Until then, only family members in the United States were permitted to send money to relatives.
- It allows the sale of some food and agricultural products to "entities independent of the Cuban government" such as restaurants, small farmers, and cooperatives. The decisions are to be made on a case-by-case basis. Only applications for sales to independent entities not controlled, owned, or operated by the Cuban government or senior party officials are eligible for consideration.
- It announces an increase in the number of charter flights to Cuba and the restoration of direct mail service to the island.
- It permits the Baltimore Orioles baseball team to arrange two exhibition baseball games with the Cuban national team, one in Cuba and one in Baltimore, as part of an effort to increase athletic, cultural, and academic exchanges. The profits from any games are to be given to Catholic relief services.

| Jan. 16, 1999 | President Clinton again suspends Title III of the Helms-Burton bill. |
| May 1999 | The Clinton administration unveils details of the regulations announced in January 1999. The new regulations allow limited sales of U.S. food and agricultural goods to private individuals and nongovernmental organizations and the expansion of travel opportunities. Universities and nongovernmental organizations in the United States may apply |

for two-year permits for travel to Cuba, which may be used by any member of the group. The amount that U.S. visitors to Cuba may spend per day is increased from $100 to $185.

July 16, 1999   President Clinton again suspends Title III of the Helms-Burton bill.

Dec. 1999   Direct charter flights between New York and Cuba begin.

Jan. 15, 2000   President Clinton again suspends Title III of the Helms-Burton bill.

Appendix B

Study Group Sessions and Participants

Susan Kaufman Purcell and J. David Rothkopf, group codirectors
Marianne Benet, group rapporteur

First Session—April 15, 1999: "Castro's Cuba: Continuity Instead of Change"
> Commentator:
> > Jaime Suchlicki, professor, North-South Center, University of Miami

> Discussant:
> > William M. LeoGrande, dean, School of Public Affairs, American University

Special Meeting—April 30, 1999
> Francisco Soberón, Minister-President, Central Bank of Cuba

Second Session—May 10, 1999: "Whither the Cuban Economy?"
> Commentator:
> > Andrew Zimbalist, professor, Economics Department, Smith College

Discussant:
Ana Julia Jatar-Hausmann, senior fellow, Inter-American Dialogue

Third Session—June 9, 1999: "U.S. Policy Toward Cuba"
Commentators:
"Why the Cuban Embargo Makes Sense in a Post–Cold War World," Susan Kaufman Purcell, vice president, Americas Society

"A Call for a Post–Cold War Cuba Policy . . . Ten Years After the End of the Cold War," David J. Rothkopf, CEO and chairman, Intellibridge Corporation

Discussant:
Richard Nuccio, visiting scholar, Weatherhead Center for International Affairs, Harvard University

Fourth Session—June 29, 1999: "After the Deluge? Cuba's Potential as a Market Economy"
Commentator:
Manuel Pastor Jr., chair, Department of Latin American and Latino Studies, University of California, Santa Cruz

Discussants:
Otto Reich, president, RMA International, Virginia
Arturo Villar, publisher, *Hispanic Market Weekly*

Special Meeting—March 22, 2000
Rev. Monsignor Carlos Manuel de Céspedes, Vicar General, Archdiocese of San Cristóbal, Havana, Cuba

Study Group Participants
Everett Ellis Briggs, Americas Society
Nestor Carbonell, PepsiCo., Inc.
Nestor Cruz, Florida Crystals
Abelardo Curdumi, Republic National Bank of New York

Mark Falcoff, American Enterprise Institute
Georges Fauriol, Center for Strategic and International Studies
José Fernández, O'Melveny & Myers LLP
Albert Fishlow, Council on Foreign Relations
Mauricio Font, Queens College
Stephen Handelman, *Time/The Toronto Star*
Rita Hauser, The Hauser Foundation
Robert Helander, Kaye, Scholer, Fierman, Hays & Handler, LLP
Marifé Hernández, The Cultural Communications Group
Lois Jackson, IBM
Roman Martínez IV, Lehman Brothers, Inc.
Kenneth Maxwell, Council on Foreign Relations
Thomas McNamara, Americas Society
Walter Russell Mead, Council on Foreign Relations
Martha Muse, The Tinker Foundation, Inc.
Mary Anastasia O'Grady, *The Wall Street Journal*
John Pearson, *Business Week*
David Pérez, Chase Capital Partners
Martín Poblete, Northeast Hispanic Catholic Center
Renate Rennie, The Tinker Foundation, Inc.
Edward Schumacher, *The Wall Street Journal Americas*
Nancy Truitt, The Tinker Foundation, Inc.

Selected Bibliography

Betancourt, Ernesto. "Governance and Post-Castro Cuba." *Cuba in Transition,* Volume 4. Washington, D.C.: Association for the Study of the Cuban Economy, 1994.

Council on Foreign Relations. *U.S.-Cuban Relations in the 21st Century.* Independent Task Force Report. New York: Council on Foreign Relations Press, 1999.

Domínguez, Jorge I. "The Secrets of Castro's Staying Power," *Foreign Affairs 72,* no. 2 (March/April 1993): 97–107.

Economist Intelligence Unit (EIU). *Country Report, Cuba.* First Quarter, 1999.

———. *Reassessing Cuba: Emerging Opportunities and Operating Challenges.* New York: EIU, 1997.

Fernández, Marzo J., José Ramón González, René Arce, and Miriaclides Daudinov. "Cuban Agriculture in the 1990s." Report prepared for the U.S.-Cuba Business Council, Arlington, Virginia, 1999.

Geyer, Georgie Ann. *Guerrilla Prince: The Untold Story of Fidel Castro.* Kansas City: Andrews McMeel, 1993.

González, Edward. *Cuba: Clearing Perilous Waters?* Santa Monica, CA: RAND, 1996.

González, Gerardo. "Transición y Recuperación Económica en Cuba," *Cuba in Transition,* Volume 7. Washington, DC: Association for the Study of the Cuban Economy, 1997, pp. 162–167.

Gunn, Gillian. *Cuba in Transition: Options for U.S. Policy.* New York: Twentieth Century Fund Press, 1993.

Horowitz, Irving L., and Jaime Suchlicki, eds. *Cuban Communism,* 9th edition. New Brunswick, NJ: Transaction Publishers, 1998.

Inter-American Dialogue. *Cuba in the Americas: Breaking the Policy Deadlock.* Washington, DC: Second Report of the Inter-American Dialogue Task Force on Cuba, September 1995.

Jatar-Hausmann, Ana Julia. *The Cuban Way: Capitalism, Communism and Confrontation.* West Hartford, CT: Kumarian Press, 1999.

Krinsky, Michael, and David Golove, eds. *U.S. Economic Measures Against Cuba.* Northampton, MA: Aletheia Press, 1993.

LeoGrande, William M. "From Havana to Miami: U.S. Cuba Policy as a Two-Level Game," *Journal of Interamerican Studies and World Affairs* 40, no. 1 (spring 1998): 67–86.

Mesa-Lago, Carmelo. "Assessing Economic and Social Performance in the Cuban Transition of the 1990s," *World Development* 26, no. 5 (1998a): 857–876.

———. "The Cuban Economy in 1997–1998: Performance and Policies." *Cuba in Transition,* Volume 8. Washington, DC: Association for the Study of the Cuban Economy, pp. 1–8.

———, ed. *Cuba After the Cold War.* Pittsburgh: University of Pittsburgh Press, 1993.

Oppenheimer, Andres. *Castro's Final Hour: The Secret Story Behind the Coming Downfall of Communist Cuba.* New York: Simon & Schuster, 1992.

Pastor, Manuel. "Cuba: The Blocked Transition." *MOCT-MOST: Economic Policy in Transitional Economies,* Volume 8, 1998, pp. 109–129.

Pastor, Manuel, and Andrew Zimbalist. "Has Cuba Turned the Corner—and If So, Which One? Macroeconomic Stabilization and the Implications for Reform in Contemporary Cuba," *Cuban Studies,* no. 27 (1997).

———. "Waiting for Change: Adjustment and Reform in Cuba," *World Development* 23, no. 5 (May 1995): 705–720.

Pérez-López, Jorge F. "Economic Reforms in a Comparative Perspective." In Jorge F. Pérez-López and Matias F. Travieso-Díaz, eds., *Perspectives on Cuban Economic Reforms.* Tempe, AZ: Center for Latin American Studies, Arizona State University, Special Studies no. 30, 1998.

———. "The Cuban Economy in the Age of Hemispheric Integration," *Journal of Interamerican Studies and World Affairs* 39, no. 3 (1997): 3–47.

———. *Cuba's Second Economy: From Behind the Scenes to Center Stage.* New Brunswick, NJ: Transaction Publishers, 1995.

Peters, Philip. *Cubans in Transition: The People of Cuba's New Economy.* Arlington, VA: Alexis de Tocqueville Institution, 1999.

Purcell, Susan Kaufman. "Cuba." In Richard N. Haass, ed. *Economic Sanctions and American Diplomacy.* New York: Council on Foreign Relations Press, 1998, chapter 2, pp. 35–56.

———. "Collapsing Cuba," *Foreign Affairs* 71, no. 1 (America and the World, February 1992): 130–145.

———. "Cuba's Cloudy Future," *Foreign Affairs* (summer 1990): 113–130.

Radu, Michael. "Cuba's Transition: Institutional Lessons from Eastern Europe," *Journal of Interamerican Studies and World Affairs* 37, no. 2 (summer 1995): 83–111.

Ritter, Archibald R. M. "Entrepreneurship, Microenterprise, and Public Policy in Cuba: Promotion, Containment, or Asphyxiation?" *Journal of Interamerican Studies and World Affairs* 40, no. 2 (1998): 63–94.

————. "The Cuban Economy in the 1990s: External Challenges and Policy Imperatives," *Journal of Interamerican Studies and World Affairs* 32 (fall 1990): 117–149.

Smith, Wayne S. "Cuba's Long Reform," *Foreign Affairs 75,* no. 2 (March/April 1996): 99–112.

Suchlicki, Jaime. "Implications of Lifting the U.S. Embargo and Travel Ban of Cuba." Center for a Free Cuba, August, 1998.

————. *Cuba: From Columbus to Castro,* 4th edition. Washington, DC, Brasseys, 1997.

————. "Cuba Without Soviet Subsidies," *Freedom Review* (January 1997): 3–7.

The Contributors

William M. LeoGrande is professor of political science in the School of Public Affairs at American University in Washington, D.C., where he has been on the faculty since 1978. He has also served as acting dean of the school and chair of the Government Department. From 1985 to 1986, he served on the staff of the Democratic Caucus Task Force on Central America of the U.S. House of Representatives. Previously, he was an international affairs fellow of the Council on Foreign Relations in New York, and worked with the Democratic Policy Committee of the U.S. Senate from 1982 to 1983.

Manuel Pastor Jr. is professor of Latin American and Latino Studies at the University of California, Santa Cruz. From 1996 to 1999 he was chair of the university's Latin American and Latino Studies Department. He previously served as associate professor of economics and director of the International and Public Affairs Center at Occidental College from 1984 to 1996. Dr. Pastor has been a Danforth fellow, a Guggenheim fellow, a Kellogg fellow, and a Fulbright fellow.

Susan Kaufman Purcell is vice president of the Americas Society and the Council of the Americas. From 1981 to 1988, she was senior fellow and director of the Latin America Project at the Council on Foreign Relations. Dr. Purcell was a Latin America specialist on

147

the U.S. State Department's policy planning staff from 1980 to 1981. Before that, she was a professor of political science at the University of California, Los Angeles. Dr. Purcell has written and edited ten books on Latin America and U.S. policy toward the region.

David J. Rothkopf is CEO and chairman of the Intellibridge Corporation (formerly known as the Newmarket Company). He is an adjunct professor of international affairs at Columbia University's School of International and Public Affairs. He was a managing director of Kissinger Associates and served as deputy undersecretary of commerce and later as acting undersecretary of commerce during the Clinton administration.

Jaime Suchlicki is the Emilio Bacardí Moreau professor of history and international studies, and director of the Institute for Cuban and Cuban American Studies at the University of Miami. For the past decade he was the editor of the *Journal of Interamerican Studies and World Affairs*. He is currently the Latin American editor for Transaction Publishers, and the author of *Cuba: From Columbus to Castro*, now in its fourth edition, and of *Mexico: From Montezuma to NAFTA* (1996). He is also a consultant to the private and public sectors on Cuba and Latin America.

Andrew Zimbalist has been professor of economics at Smith College since 1974. From 1992 to 1994, he chaired the Latin American Scholars Association's Task Force on Scholarly Relations with Cuba. Dr. Zimbalist was a visiting professor at Doshisha University in Kyoto, Japan, in 1985, and a research fellow at Harvard University in 1980. He has consulted in Latin America for the United Nations Development Programme, the U.S. Agency for International Development, and numerous private companies. Dr. Zimbalist has published several dozen articles and twelve books.

Index

149

70; private sector, 5; resistance
to change, 65–66; socialism, 3;
Soviet support for, 83; U.S.
political debate over, ix, 117–
120
Castro, Raúl: civil society, 72;
Communist Party and, 67;
departure of, 7, 76–77;
ideological purity, 12*n3;* internal
security, 71; militarization of the
economy, 60; military loyalty to,
69–70, 75; as successor to Fidel,
66, 68, 123–124
Catholic Church, 6, 72, 94, 129
Ceauşescu, Nicolae, 92
Central Bank, 40
Central Europe, 110
Chávez, Hugo, 77, 78, 111
China: persistence of communist
government in, 74; reform
model, 62–63, 128; solidarity
with Cuba, 78; special economic
zones, 62; U.S. relations with,
113, 120, 122; Western
engagement with, 91–92; WTO
membership, 123
Chrétien, Jean, 95
Cienfuegos, Osmani, 66
Cimex, 24
Citrus fruits, 45–46
Civil society, 71–73, 84, 90
Clinton, Bill, 86–87, 88, 118–119,
135–136; administration, 78, 90,
97, 123
Cold War, 1, 107–108
Colombia: Cuban support for
guerrillas in, 77, 78, 84, 111;
narco-traffic threat to U.S., 113;
trade with Cuba, 63
Common Market of the South
(Mercosur), 47
Communist Party of Cuba:
international influence of, 106;
lack of importance of, 66–67;
military role in, 67, 69;
monolithic nature of, 59;
orthodox thinking in, 66; popular
disillusionment with, 57

Concilio Cubano, 73
Confederación de Trabajadores de
Cuba (CTC), 73
Consumer goods, 61
Containment policy, 84, 108
Cooperatives: agricultural, 13, 18,
33, 35; benefits of, 27;
ownership rights, 50;
productivity of, 53*n5*
Corruption, 23, 43
Costa Rica, 128
Council of State, 75–76
Council on Foreign Relations, 101,
106
Cuba: geographical size of, 108;
population of, 108; world
ranking of economy, 107
Cuban Democracy Act of *1992. See*
Torricelli bill
Cuban Liberty and Democratic
Solidarity (Libertad) Act of
1996. See Helms-Burton bill
Cuban American National
Foundation (CANF), 97–98,
100–101, 121
Cuban Americans: Elián González
case, 107; embargo, support for,
97–101, 117; European heritage
of, 39; as investors in Cuba, 39,
50, 51–52, 131; political
influence of, 10, 97, 106–107,
117–118; political party
identification of, 118–119,
125*n9;* potential control of
Cuban economy by, 27, 39, 43,
131; remittances to Cuba, 9–10,
18, 28*n8,* 48–49, 83, 131, 137

D'Amato, Alfonse, 97
Defense Intelligence Agency, U.S.,
106
Democratic Party (U.S.), 118,
125*n9*
Deng Xiaoping, 74
Dissidents, 36, 66, 73, 77–78. *See
also* Repression
Dole, Bob, 118
Dollars, U.S.: bonuses paid in, 19;

About the Book

Though few observers dispute that change is coming to Cuba, there is a notable lack of consensus regarding the pace and direction of that change. The authors of this collection offer a range of views on the growing political and economic challenges facing the Castro regime, how those challenges will be met, and Cuba's prospects for a peaceful transition to democracy. The book also includes two strongly opposing assessments of the nature, impact, desirability, and sustainability of the U.S. embargo against Cuba.

Susan Kaufman Purcell is vice president of the Americas Society and Council of the Americas. **David J. Rothkopf** is CEO and chairman of Intellibridge Corporation.